# The Transforming Gospel

## The Mission of François Coillard and Basuto Evangelists in Barotseland

Jean-François Zorn

Translated by Dora Atger
Edited by Elizabeth Visinand-Fernie

WCC Publications, Geneva

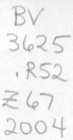
This is a translation of chapter 2, part 3, of *Le grand Siècle d'une mission protestante: La Mission de Paris de 1822 à 1914*, by Jean-François Zorn, édition Karthala – Les Bergers et Les Mages, Paris, 1993.

Cover design: Marie Arnaud Snakkers

ISBN 2-8254-1425-5

© 2004, World Council of Churches
150, route de Ferney, P.O. Box 2100
1211 Geneva 2, Switzerland
Web site: http://www.wcc-coe.org

Printed in France

# TABLE OF CONTENTS

# FOREWORD

The United Church of Zambia welcomes the publication of the history of the work of François Coillard and the Basuto Evangelists among the Lozi people of the western part of Zambia. The United Church of Zambia will forever be indebted to the author, Dr J. F. Zorn, for this history of the Church. We greatly appreciate his kind permission to have this work translated and published. It was very much needed so as to enable Zambian Christians and other English-speaking people to have access to the story of the work of the heroic men and women involved, many of whom sacrificed their lives in this mission.

This book is written by a French Reformed theologian, historian and missiologist. He is qualified to write this history because he has his roots in French Protestantism and is familiar with the work of Paris Mission

The Church faces the risk of forgetting. It is interesting to see that the Bible does not take the human mind for granted, both in the Old and the New Testament. We find numerous reminders to God's people to recall always God's actions in and through the lives of his people in the past. As soon as Israel came out of Egypt reminders were given to the people in the form of the Ten Commandments and feasts or festivals. They were commanded to pass on the History to their children.

The work of François Coillard and the Basuto Evangelists is bound to suffer oblivion if the next generations are not given the history of their religious roots. What compounds this situation is the fact that most of the literature on the work of PMS exists only in French.

Church history helps us to affirm and celebrate the work of past leaders. It also inspires us with a sense of gratitude and thankfulness to God, for it has been said - and rightly so - that history is His story. It is not only an account of heroic men and women, but an account of God's work in and through them. A student of Church history therefore reads with enthusiasm and anticipation, expecting to see God's acts among his people. In addition, Church history, and lessons of the past, whether negative or positive, inspire us in our mission today.

This story is about a heroic mission. Coillard and his group came to Barotseland at a time when King Lewanika's kingdom was going through a political crisis, faced with civil war. The missionaries had to contend with cultural and traditional beliefs and practices which were very different from theirs. They came to a totally new and alien culture. The environment was hostile. There were no roads. They slept in tents for there were no permanent houses like they were used to in Europe. They had to contend with tropical diseases like malaria. A number of them died and are buried at Mwandi Mission or Sefula. This history therefore is a story of their heroic faith; the risks they took, the sacrifices made and their passion for Christ and their love for the Lozi people.

Today, nearly a 119 years later, mission in Barotseland is still an unfinished task. There are areas where the Church has not penetrated or where its presence is not felt. Areas like Mashi, Sinjembela, Sioma and other areas of Shangombo District, Shekela, Sikongo, Mampolomoka, Nyengo-Makoma of Kalabo District. Still others are Lukulu, parts of Kaoma, Senanga East and the forest areas of Mongu (Makanda). In some of these areas the Church exists, albeit in no significant way.

Even in areas where the Paris Mission had a strong presence, new mission challenges have arisen. Issues of HIV/AIDS, poverty, unemployment among others. It is hoped that the reading of this history will help the Church to renew its passion for missions.

Did the Gospel make an impact on the ma-Lozi people? King Litia's address to the Lozi people on March 15, 1916 states it clearly: "Education and the preaching of the Gospel - therein lies the salvation of the country..." (C.W. Mackintosh, *The New Zambezi Trail: A Record of Two Journeys to North-Western Rhodesia*, London, Marshall Brothers, 1922). And F. Coillard in 1903, a year before he died, wrote in his will: "On the threshold of eternity and in the presence of my God, I solemnly bequeath to the Churches of France, my native land, the responsibility of the Lord's work in Batroseland and I adjure them, in His Holy Name, never to give it up - which would be to despise and renounce the rich harvest reserved to the sowing they have accompanied in suffering and in tears" (Edward Shillito, *François Coillard: A Wayfaring Man*, London, SCM, 1923).

This book is not for historians or Church leaders only, it is intended for all Christians of all Church traditions. It is sent out with hope and prayer that even in our generation we will see a renewed interest, faith and commitment for mission. May this book from a Christian in the North, contribute to the increase of his Kingdom and His glory in the South.

*Synod Bishop M.P. Siyemeto*

# AUTHOR'S PREFACE

The Zambezi (or Barotseland) mission, founded in 1885, was the fourth mission field of the Société des Missions Évangéliques de Paris (Paris Missionary Society - PMS). This mission society was itself founded in 1822 with the help of the London Missionary Society (LMS). From 1829 it began working in southern Africa, where it founded its mission to Lesotho (Basutoland) in 1833 and Senegal (West Africa) in 1863. Why did a French-speaking mission society1 become involved in the early 19th century in an area like southern Africa, where France had no colonial interests?

First of all, contrary to what is generally believed, Protestant missions have not systematically followed in the wake of colonisation, but often preceded it and subsequently objected to it. But there is another reason: in France in the early 19th century, Catholicism was dominant, so Protestants were not free to engage in mission in countries under French protectorate. Before being able to send their own missionaries anywhere in the world, the founders of the PMS provided the churches which supported it with information on the missionaries of other societies, including those of LMS, and prayed for them. Then the LMS directors, including John Philip, the superintendent for southern Africa, proposed to their counterparts at PMS that they send French missionaries to South Africa. In the Cape Colony there had already been Huguenots2 of French origin since the 17th century. These Huguenots had fled persecution in their homeland, taking refuge first in the Netherlands, from whence they were sent to South Africa.

The PMS accepted this plan, and French missionaries arrived in the Cape Colony in 1829. But they did not come as pastors to their French cousins who had become Afrikaner Boer colonists, because the latter were already applying a policy of racial separation, which the missionaries condemned. Their intention was to meet 'real black pagans' and evangelise them. So they moved on in search of a mission field, settling to the north of the Cape Colony in the Sotho country, invited by the Sotho chief Moshoeshoe who, according to the tradition of that era, wanted white missionaries to come and help him build his nation.

Thus the Lesotho mission was founded in 1833, with its first stations at Morija and Thaba Bosiu. It was successful and further stations were quickly founded. The indigenous church continued to grow until the conflicts between the British and the Boers interfered with the relative independence, which the British protectorate had granted to Moshoeshoe.

This caused a Christian uprising against the PMS missionaries; they were accused suddenly of having facilitated the colonisation of their country. The second generation of PMS missionaries in Lesotho, after 1850, thus had to fight against the colonial ambitions of both the Boers and the British in Lesotho, and show that they were still supporters of a Sotho state in the colonial context and of a Sotho church within the missionary context. To achieve this the Church of Lesotho had to have its own mission field. This idea first occurred to a Swiss PMS missionary in Lesotho, Adolphe Mabille, and was carried out thanks to the dynamic leadership of another PMS missionary, the Frenchman François Coillard. It was he who founded the Zambezi mission as a daughter church of the Church of Lesotho. How did this come about?

The little book you are about to read (an extract from The Great Century of a Protestant Mission: the Paris Mission Society from 1822-1914) tells the extraordinary story of this mission, created in Africa under the joint direction of Europeans and Africans. The expedition led by François Coillard, which set out for the Zambezi in January 1864 and arrived at the great river in August 1885, in fact included some twenty people, a majority of whom were Africans (Sotho, Pedi, Lozi). But it was not the first of its kind in the region. Since David Livingstone had explored the course of the Zambezi in 1851, there had been a steady stream of European missionaries accompanied by African evangelists.

What Coillard and his co-workers were planning, however, was very special. They wanted the Church of Lesotho to have its own mission field, just as the churches of France had formerly had their own mission fields. The French churches' mission field was that of Lesotho, as described above. Coillard had explored the Lozi country on the Zambezi for the Church of Lesotho on a previous expedition in 1877-1879. He had come to the conclusion that there were ethnic and linguistic ties between the Lozi and the Sotho peoples, a good reason for the Sotho to bring the Gospel to the Lozi.

You will read of the many obstacles encountered by this venture. Without Coillard's determination it would never have succeeded. Neither the churches of Lesotho, nor especially those in France, Switzerland and Italy, supporters of the PMS, were very enthusiastic about it. But it was carried forward by Coillard's faith, and the conviction grew little by little that the project was indeed an obedient response to the Lord's call. The route was arduous and caused many deaths, which is why it is considered, among the PMS missions, as a 'heroic mission'. The book ends with the year 1914, but the story goes on. For the more recent past there are probably still living witnesses who could tell it, but it should doubtless also be written down one day.

I want to underline in conclusion that, while the PMS may have seemed opposed to Coillard's plan to found a mission on the Zambezi, it was not due to a lack of missionary conviction, even less to a lack of Christian faith. Certainly there were some members of the PMS Committee who did not think missionary activity should be pursued in countries under British control, such as Basutoland and Barotseland, although since the Berlin conference on Africa (1884-85), no colonial nation was allowed to hinder Christian missions3. Thus French Protestants could go wherever they wished, and indeed certain countries were calling for them. But despite these calls, to Gabon in 1891, New Caledonia in 1892, Madagascar in 1896, then to Cameroon and Togo after World War I, to all of which the PMS responded, it never abandoned the mission on the Zambezi, and supported it all the way to church autonomy in 19744. All these mission fields, now churches in their own right, together make up the CEVAA (Community of Churches in Mission), which succeeded and replaced the PMS in 1971. Thus the plea in Coillard's testament written in March 1903, imploring the churches of France never to abandon those of Barotseland, was carried out. Better yet, today a much wider community of churches than those of France and the former PMS sustains the Church in Zambia, so that it can continue its mission.

*Jean-François Zorn*
*Protestant Institute of Theology*
*University of Montpellier, France*

# INTRODUCTION

Mission history considers 1885 as the foundation year of the Zambezi Mission. On August 23, an expedition coming from Lesotho, led by François Coillard, crossed the Zambezi River. Having waited a whole year at Leshoma, on the right bank of the river, the expedition was finally able to move into the Lozi country and set up an outpost near an important local chief's stronghold, used to observe Matebele troop movements. In the 1820s, the Kololo, a Sotho group, had migrated northwards. The plan for a mission to the Zambezi dated back to the 1860s. The 1885 expedition was the fourth attempt in 20 years to reach the area from Lesotho. Hermann Dieterlen writes that the idea had long been in the mind of the missionary Adolphe Mabille: the evangelisation of Africa and the participation of the Lesotho churches in that great task.

In 1862, an attempt had been made by sending the evangelist, Esaia Seele, to the Transvaal. But a four-year war (1864-1868) had prevented the Lesotho missionaries from following in the footsteps of the African pioneer. Despite the setbacks, the project of a Lesotho church mission abroad never left Mabille's mind. Ten years after Seele, he organised with Paul Berthoud a first expedition to the Spelonken (N. Transvaal) where the Swiss mission had started a station in 1875. Shortly after this, the Zambezi project came into being. Two events were instrumental in this decision:

The Board of Directors of the Paris Mission refused to support the Spelonken Mission because it meant working with a population subject to the Boers. It preferred to sponsor a mission among the independent populations on the banks of the Limpopo and beyond.

The Sotho evangelist Asser Sehahoubane, whom Mabille and Berthoud had settled in the Transvaal, returned to Lesotho in October 1874 and convinced the Mission Conference, meeting at Hermon in February 1875, to undertake the evangelisation of the Nyaï country beyond the Limpopo, since the chiefs were asking for missionaries.

The same Hermon Conference decided to send a second expedition under the guidance of Hermann Dieterlen, a young missionary recently arrived in Lesotho. It was accepted by the Board, but for reasons explained below, the expedition fell through.

In November 1876, the Board decided on a third expedition to be led by François Coillard. After two years of exploration (1877-78) which led him to the Zambezi, Coillard came back convinced that the Lozi country on the upper reaches of the Zambezi was where missionaries were needed. Yet it took another six years before a fourth attempt led to the founding of the Zambezi Mission. Why this long delay?

Tragic events had dogged the members of the third expedition. These events so discouraged the Mission Conference and the Lesotho churches, and also shocked some sectors of French Protestantism, that the Paris Board hesitated to support a new attempt. However, the adventurous missionaries were far from discouraged and had the support of other sectors of Protestantism beyond the national boundaries. Their daring was galvanised by these obstacles and they never looked back, despite the death of several members of the expeditions.

At this point, the 'Mission to the Zambezi', originally carefully planned to be a 'second Lesotho', gradually developed into something different. Danger and even death were no longer considered as misfortunes (such as those that had led to relinquishing Senegal), but as tribulations to be met with courage and faith. Thus a new type of missionary was born, a conquering Christian hero, hitherto unknown in the Paris Mission.

Examined below is how this new direction compelled the Paris Mission to renew its thinking and its apostolic practices, and in what way European Protestantism, torn between the enthusiasts and the reticent, the nationalists and universalists, either supported the venture or threatened to withdraw from it.

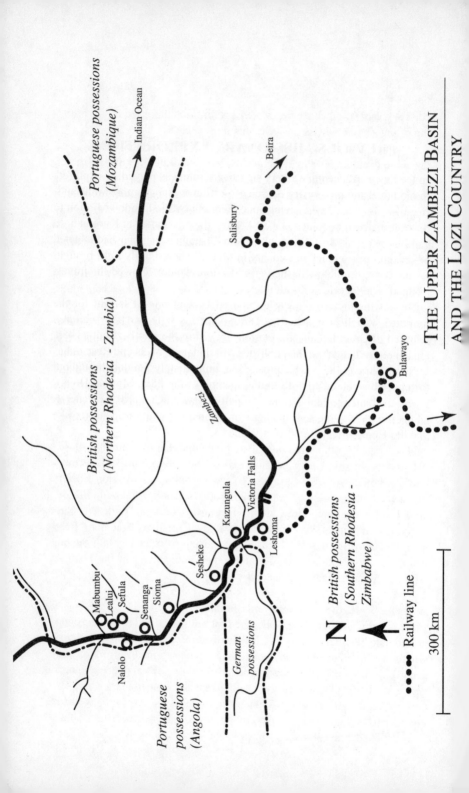

THE UPPER ZAMBEZI BASIN
AND THE LOZI COUNTRY

Portuguese possessions (Mozambique)

Indian Ocean

Beira

Salisbury

British possessions (Northern Rhodesia - Zambia)

Bulawayo

Zambezi

Kazungula

Victoria Falls

Sesheke

Leshoma

British possessions (Southern Rhodesia - Zimbabwe)

Mabumbu
Lealui
Sefula
Senanga
Sioma

Nalolo

German possessions

Portuguese possessions (Angola)

N

Railway line

300 km

# I

# PREVIOUS MISSIONARY EXPLORATIONS

In the nineteenth century a very significant role was played by explorers in moulding the missionary conscience of Europeans, the most outstanding of whom was David Livingstone. Sent out by the London Mission to Southern Africa, he joined Robert Moffat, the missionary at Kuruman. In 1844 he married Moffat's daughter Mary. Another daughter had married Jean Frédoux, a French missionary in Motito. These family links brought Livingstone in touch with the Paris Mission, which followed the travels of the missionary doctor with interest.

It was his father-in-law who advised Livingstone to set out for the Zambezi, which he reached in 1851. After his wife and four children returned to Great Britain, Livingstone stayed in the Zambezi until 1856. On his return to Europe, he published Missionary Travels and Researches in South Africa (1857) which made him immediately famous throughout Europe. This coincided with the re-opening of the Paris Mission House, where Coillard and Mabille met. "Together", wrote Coillard "we venerated the pioneers of the Lesotho Mission as on a par with missionaries like van der Kemp, Moffat and John Williams."

Posted to Lesotho, both men shared the hope that the churches of that country might discover a mission call of their own. On 31 December 1862, Mabille wrote to Casalis: "I so wish our Paris Mission Society could send a few missionaries to the Sesotho-speaking Makololo discovered by Livingstone. They are in fact, true Basutos. With the New Testament in hand and accompanied by a few Christians from here, I feel sure the enterprise would be feasible... starting from Senegal on the one hand, and from Lesotho on the other, they could meet in the heart of Africa... What a gigantic project it would be."

## A. Esaïa Seele, the first Sotho missionary

Little is known about Esaïa Seele, the first Sotho sent out to be a missionary outside his own country. A Christian from Berea in Lesotho, a church where a Christianising movement had recently occurred, "He was" according to Coillard, "of a high social position, of exceptional intelligence and had a pleasant nature; he could speak English, French and several native languages and had extensive medical knowledge." So many qualities united in a single person might lead one to suspect that Coillard had idealised him. Whether this was the case or not, the fact that he became the first Sotho missionary was mentioned systematically by Coillard whenever he recalled the origins of the Mission to the Zambezi.

Coillard's intention was to underline that this foreign mission was the business of the churches of Lesotho and that they had, as well, men of the right calibre for such an undertaking. During the war years in Lesotho and the exile of the missionaries, the Berlin Mission continued support of Seele's evangelising work among the Pedi.

## B. The spark that was Asser (1873)

Ten years after this first attempt, Asser, a new man left in the Transvaal by Berthoud and Mabille, answered the missionaries' call to investigate whether a door of opportunity might not open for the Sothos between the Limpopo and the Zambezi.

In his first book published in 1899, On the upper reaches of the Zambezi, the title of which resembled Livingstone's book, Coillard praised Asser in terms similar to those used for Seele: "He showed the same shrewdness and was remarkably observant. He kept a journal, noting any details that he thought might interest us or be of use later ... Three chiefs seemed particularly keen to have missionaries."

When Asser returned to Lesotho in October 1874, his testimony caused an electric shock, wrote Coillard. Mabille informed the Paris Board "We have before us a door opened wide by the Lord. Who will seize the opportunity? Many objections will be made. It's too far away, they'll say. Yes, true, but it's in the right direction, we shan't be stepping on anyone's toes ... and we shall reach the Zambezi and extend a hand of friendship to the central tribes that need evangelising."

The following mission conferences at Hermon (February 1875) and Morija (August 1875) decided that the Lesotho churches would send four new evangelists to the Nyaï people. However, on learning that the Transvaal government would not let Sothos cross their territory, the Berea conference in January 1876 suggested that a missionary should accompany them. Mabille and Coillard volunteered but Hermann Dieterlen, a missionary newly-arrived from Alsace, was chosen by the Conference. The expedition was co-directed by Asser and made up of two other Sotho evangelists, Andreas and Onesima, and two wagon drivers Elias and Liboke, twenty-two people in all, including wives and children. To signal the ecclesiastical nature of the mission, the expedition was given a formal send-off by the Leribe synod in April 1876.

## C. A door closes on Hermann Dieterlen (1876)

This expedition, the first of its kind for the Paris Mission, was presented to the Protestant public of France as a perilous 'indigenous enterprise'. Dieterlen was called 'a valiant son of our unfortunate Alsace'. The same theme would later be applied to Madagascar as being the missionary conquest compensating for the loss for France in 1870 of Alsace and Lorraine. Similarly, Coillard compared the departure of Dieterlen and his companions to that of Sebetoane who, "45 years earlier led his clan north, to found his powerful kingdom in the unknown upper reaches of the Zambezi". It is evident that these speeches were designed to exalt the mission undertaken by peaceful Christian explorers, black and white, as against the caravans of adventurers in search of slaves, or of those who, under the pretext of driving out slave-traders, traded in arms and liquor.

On reaching Pretoria, however, the members of Dieterlen and Asser's expedition were arrested (May 1876). The Sotho evangelists were thrown in jail and Dieterlen was lucky to be bailed out by a German missionary. Morija and Paris railed against the State of the Transvaal which called itself 'Christian and civilised' yet arrested messengers of peace. Nevertheless: "the Gospel entered Europe through a prison", wrote Coillard on 15 June 1876, after the expedition returned to Lesotho: "The Lord is Almighty and All-Wisdom... the watchword the English evangelist Moody gave to all the Christians of Europe on leaving them was the word that rings more than ever in the mission fields of Africa: Forward! Forward!"

## D. François Coillard's expedition (1877-1879)

The failure of Hermann Dieterlen and his companions' mission did not break the spirit of the Lesotho churches nor of the Conference. The latter met at Thaba Bossiu on November 28, 1876 and was concerned "not to discourage the Banyai people who were waiting impatiently for the missionaries they had been promised, nor to dampen the zeal of the Lesotho churches." A new attempt to reach the Nyaï country was decided upon. But the death of Louis Cochet, Dieterlen's neighbour at Bethesda, on October 9, 1876, prevented the Conference from commissioning him to lead it. Coillard was preparing to return to Europe on leave; due to illness he had been absent from the conference, but he was asked to take charge.

"This proposal struck me like lightning" wrote Coillard in his journal. But it was not a fatal blow; rather, it was like a shock that renewed his Christian vocation. He likened it to Paul's experience on the road to Damascus or Luther's on the way to Erfurt. Ten days later, Coillard and his wife were able to "resist the counsels of flesh and blood and once again say to God: Here we are Lord, do with us what you will".

The Board in Paris consented to the proposals of the Conference and said how moved they were by the self-sacrifice of the Coillards. Nevertheless, once again it meant that mission friends and the churches of France had to be persuaded to adopt the projected exploration beyond the Limpopo River. The interest could not measure up to the enthusiasm shown by outside scientific and political groups for an expedition into the heart of Africa. A persistent annual deficit forced the Committee to increase its public information.

In early 1877, the churches of France were visited by Charles Malan, an unemployed British Army officer. He happened to be the grandson of César Malan (1787-1864), a revivalist preacher and pastor of an independent church in Geneva. Malan, according to Maurice Leenhardt, was like a knight-crusader committed to the religious conquest of Southern Africa. He visited all Paris Mission stations in Lesotho and returned to Europe convinced of their calling to evangelise the heart of Africa.

After a trip of several weeks visiting churches in Lyon, Valence, Marseille, Nîmes, Pau, Bordeaux and Saintes, he spoke at the Oratory of the Louvre in Paris: "You are among the first ranks of the pioneers of the Gospel" he told the churches of France. "You have men ready and waiting; however you must help and encourage them. This is something the churches of France don't know how to do as they should. They have not yet understood the glorious privilege which the Lord is granting them".

The JDME published a letter from Hermann Dieterlen in which he pointed out the link between the projected missionary expedition and the parallel enterprises of explorers of the time. "It seems to me," he wrote to the President of the Paris Mission on 22 February "that our enterprise north of the Limpopo could and should become a claim to fame for France in the concert of civilised nations. Ever since the Geographic Congress of Brussels, countless travellers will find their way to the unknown countries around the Great Lakes and the high plateaux… but it is less likely that they will tackle the countries between the Limpopo and the Zambezi. It might be that some French missionaries will be given the opportunity to explore these unknown countries, said to be so rich and so beautiful, in order to reveal their resources… we shall be known as the missionaries of Jesus Christ, whose only ambition is to faithfully fulfil our task… But if, at one and the same time, we are able to be of service to science and our country, it would be a great mistake to miss the opportunity of doing so, and to deliberately restrict our field of action."

Dieterlen greatly regretted not being part of the expedition. Nevertheless, his arrest in Pretoria had roused a wave of sympathy for France in southern Africa. The protests of the French Consul and the English government, the criticism in the colonial press, had made the Transvaal Government think twice, Dieterlin wrote on 22 February. As a result, the President made no difficulty about granting permission for the French missionaries and Sotho evangelists to pass through the country. Then, on 12 April 1877, the Transvaal came under British control, ending several years of conflict between the Pedi and the Boers. Thus, on 18 April, heading an expedition of some twenty people, Coillard set out for the Nyaï country through a pacified region. Three men, Asser Sehahoubane, Asaele and Andreas and their families, participants in the previous expedition, set out in three wagons, each drawn by sixteen oxen. Two evangelists accompanied them: Aaron Mayoro and Eleazar Marathane and three other young men: Bushman, Khosana and Fono. European participants were Coillard and his wife Christina, née Mackintosh, and their niece Elise Coillard who had joined them at Leribe shortly before their departure.

The expedition lasted more than two years, from April 1877 to July 1879. It progressed rapidly till it reached the domain of chief Masonda in the heart of the Nyaï country, after a welcome stop-over in Valdezia among the Swiss missionaries. However, in August 1877 problems arose. When Coillard refused to give Masonda gunpowder, his troops encircled Coillard and threatened the expedition, so that the wagons could hardly move on; but he was able to reach Chief Malinakobe, Masonda's brother, who seemed more willing to welcome the missionaries. They were soon to discover, however, that the Nyaïs were not independent and had to pay tribute to Lobengula, Moslikatse's son, the great chief of the Ndebeles. Colliard could not therefore settle in the area without the approval of Lobengula, who lived in Bulawayo, 100 km away. Asser was sent ahead and only returned two months later, bringing with him an order for the expedition to appear in Bulawayo, under escort, as prisoners of the great chief.

On arrival in Bulawayo, Coillard met some missionaries from the London Mission Society who, without much success, had been settled there for the last twenty years. From 15 December 1877 till 4 March 1878, the expedition was held up. Lobengula accused the Lesotho missionaries of not being official envoys from Letsie, and for coming from the district of Molapo which had helped the British capture Langalibalili, an Ndebele chief. The result of interviews with Lobengula meant that

Coillard and his companions were forbidden to settle in either the land of the Nyaï or of the Ndebele.

On 5 March 1878, Coillard wrote to the Board in Paris that the only alternative was to return to Lesotho or to attempt another settlement elsewhere. The thought of returning to Lesotho seemed to him "a temptation from the enemy and a cowardly let-down". Despite a certain degree of discouragement, all the members of the expedition shared this feeling. Regretfully, he considered retreating with his group to Shoshong, somewhere between Lesotho and the Zambezi, (the nearest village with postal services) to await instructions from the Conference and the Board. The latter part of the letter gave information obtained from Kololo refugees which "directed his thoughts irresistibly towards the country of the Malozis beyond the Zambezi".

These thoughts were not new, and Coillard was conscious of the fact that going to the Zambezi was a gigantic enterprise, necessitating a long and perilous journey, the end of which would still be unknown. But he was determined: "As for us, we have at heart the extension of our Saviour's Kingdom and our lives count as nothing. We are certain that our Lesotho brothers, you, gentlemen of the Board, and the friends who support us, are all at one with us in this great task." The second part of this letter does not appear in the JDME. Did the Board and the Conference disapprove of the project, even though it had been planned long before?

During its meeting on 22 July, 1878, the Board examined the report of the Mission Conference of Lesotho which had met two months earlier at Mabulela and agreed that Coillard, on returning from Shoshong, "was to look for a field of work on the northern border of the Transvaal, which could serve also as an observation post. They should wait there for the Lord to open the door hitherto closed".

The Board and the Conference informed Coillard in writing of their decision; but by 27 April the expedition had already arrived at Shoshong after a journey made more difficult by the lack of water and during which several members fell ill. They were warmly welcomed by the Hepburns, a missionary couple from the London Missionary Society and by Khama, the Christian chief of the Ngwatos. It was there that Coillard awaited the letters from Lesotho and from France. In spite of strong bouts of fever and warnings from the Hepburns, Coillard was impatient, avidly gathering any information which might hasten an eventual departure towards the Zambezi. Even Chief Khama took part in the plans, going so far (on 23 May) as to send a delegation of five people ahead to the Lozi chief, to help open the way.

On May 29, Coillard wrote in his diary: "I keep wondering what news will come from Lesotho. Will the order be given to return immediately or will we be free to follow the call of Providence? I tremble to think. My heart's desire is to move on and bring the Good News to these tribes who do not know the Saviour. My heart throbs to think of it. The sacrifice of my life would seem as nothing to that." In the absence of the long-awaited letters, Coillard decided that the expedition could no longer wait. On 8 June he wrote to the Board: "Our aim is not to found a mission but to explore the possibilities. We are going off as scouts, and if God brings us back in good health we shall tell what we have seen and it will be for you to say what should be done."

This letter appeared in the JDME of September 1878 together with 14 pages of comments from the Board. "We admire and tremble and bow before so firm a faith, such complete devotion, yet we wonder whether M. Coillard was truly called to undertake further exploration into such perilous regions." After thinking over the solutions put forward by Coillard, the Board concluded: "Whatever happens, we have before us M. and Mme Coillard and their three faithful companions (in fact the three evangelists Asser, Asaele, Eleazar and Khosana, one of the boys, together with Elise Coillard, their niece). They have left despite the danger. May God bless them and keep them; may they be spared the fevers, that enemy hitherto unknown to their brothers in southern Africa."

By the end of July the expedition had reached Leshoma and on 1 July the Zambezi was in sight. One of Khama's messengers who was already there told them he had not been able to reach the Lozi country on account of recent political disorders which had led Chief Robosi to eliminate all his vassals. Coillard, together with Asser and Eleazar, successfully crossed the Zambezi using the canoes the local chiefs had lent them. In a letter dated 30 August 1878 which reached Paris only in January 1879, Coillard explained: "The fact that I was a missionary, a profession that Livingstone had so honoured, served as a passport. Whether I like it or not I am a 'Ngaka', a doctor, a successor to Livingstone. This means that any missionary who comes along steps into the shoes of that giant. Sesotho is spoken and understood; it is the means of communication between different tribes that have their own dialect." Coillard was thus able to confirm that the Kololos had truly been exterminated by the Lozi, that Sotho was still understood and that the arrival of Sotho evangelists seemed to raise no problems among the Lozi population.

But serious difficulties awaited the newcomers: the message and the gifts sent to Robosi had not reached him. So Coillard and his companions went back to Leshoma on 4 September. On the 13th Khosana fell ill and died. Seeing that their supplies were diminishing, Coillard sent Eleazar to Sesheke on the 20th. Still without news a month later, Coillard decided with Asser to return to Sesheke. On 1 November, he learnt from reliable sources that Robosi had finally received and understood the message, but having only recently acceded to the throne, he could not welcome the missionaries in the best conditions. "Should you wish to leave the country before the rainy season, go in peace and come back in April." Coillard hoped to put this invitation to the test, but a message from his wife told him that famine was rife at Leshoma and that the Portuguese explorer Serpa Pinto, whose life Coillard had saved a few weeks before, was ill and at death's door. Torn between the duty of assisting his own people and the hope of an interview with Robosi, Coillard waited. But on 5 November, Eleazar having died of fever, Coillard and Asser returned to Leshoma from whence, on 13 November, the expedition made its way back to Lesotho, reaching Shoshong on 31 December.

On the way, they heard three distressing items of news: the Paris Mission was in deficit (over the 70.000 francs limit), so the Board was reluctant to maintain support for the Zambezi project; the Conference disapproved of the project and suggested Coillard should return to the Spelonken to consider a new field of work to be suggested by the Swiss missionaries; Khosana who had stayed at Shoshong due to ill-health, had died.

Coillard was now at a loss "Were I alone, there would be no hesitation. I carry the Barotsis in my heart," he wrote in his journal on 18 January 1879. Then a letter from Mabille confirmed that he too was in favour of the mission, but the evangelists wanted them to go to Spelonken. So Coillard, despite his reservations, agreed to accompany them.

On 29 March 1879, the expedition reached Valdezia. The search for a new mission field came to an abrupt halt. The station at Mochane which the Swiss missionaries had hoped for, was claimed by the Berlin Mission Society and the local queen refused to meet Coillard. Finally, the Hepburns suggested to the evangelists Asser, Aaron, Asaele and Andreas that they settle on the station at Seleka in the LMS area, whose chief was a vassal of Khama, and they accepted this proposal. On 22 April Coillard took leave of the evangelists, convinced that their undertaking was a first step towards the Nyaï area or the land of the Barotsi.

On its part, the Board took note that exploring the Transvaal field, as suggested by them, went against Coillard's convictions and that he was more than ever convinced, as were the evangelists, that the area was closed and that they should turn their attention towards the Zambezi.

On July 15, the expedition crossed the Caledon and returned to Lesotho. On 1 August the executive commissions of the Synod and the Conference met in Morija to hear Coillard's report and consider what follow-up to give to the Zambezi Mission. Coillard gave his report and summed up his feelings in his journal: "As for the mission to the Barotses, all the missionaries were reluctant except for Mabille. It seems quite impossible to them, especially on account of the fevers. I begged them to let me return to the Zambezi, but they refused categorically. They want me to return to Europe, to reach an agreement with the Board in Paris and, if possible, to interest the churches in work that gets no sympathy here. In fact, I am held totally responsible. It is clear that there is a misunderstanding between the Board in Paris and us. These gentlemen seem to think that the Zambezi Mission has to be indigenous; they seem to think that we have the funds and the men on the spot. This is not the case. And will the French, who cannot reduce their deficit, supply us with the resources of men and money needed? I certainly appreciated the spirit in which the discussions were held, but am saddened by the conclusions they reached." These conclusions are recorded in a letter Hermann Dieterlen wrote to the Board in the name of the Conference. He pointed out the considerable differences between the initial project of evangelising the Banaïs and that of founding mission work among the Barotsis:

-	The great distance (1600 km) between the Lozi country and Lesotho meant that the Zambezi project could not depend on the Sotho churches;
-	The difficult health conditions of the Lozi country and the dangers involved in the enterprise required financial resources beyond the means of the Lesotho church;
-	The founding of the mission could not reasonably be left solely to native evangelists.

To conclude, François Coillard was encouraged to plead his Zambezi cause in Europe, "as it is no longer a question of work depending on the Lesotho churches and the Mission Conference, but rather a new responsibility that the Board would undertake and support, and to which the Lesotho churches and the Conference would contribute according to their means, either in men or money". François and Christina Coillard therefore left Lesotho on 19 November 1879, having first helped Paul-Amos Dormoy and his wife, their successors, to settle in at Leribe. But the 'war of guns' had just begun in the country…

## II

## COILLARD'S JOURNEY TO EUROPE
## STIRS POPULAR RESPONSE (1880-1882)

### A. Report to the Board: Agreement on a fourth exploration to the Zambezi

The Coillards were received by the Board in Paris at a formal reception on 15 March 1880, then on 5 April to present their report on the Zambezi Mission project. On 3 May, the Board decided to print a brochure including Coillard's report, the opinion of the Board explained by Georges Appia, and an appeal to the churches written by Alfred Boegner.

The opening sentence of the Coillard's report declared: "The missionary spirit is a spirit of aggression and conquest. Further, always further, is our motto". It put an end to the idea that the Zambezi might be a purely Lesotho churches-led mission. True, the "indigenous aspect would predominate" but Coillard asked for at least "two ordained missionaries, and if possible, one or two European artisans" and noted on three occasions that they should be prepared to replace those who might succumb in this 'post of honour', and whose graves, like those of the evangelists Eleazar and Khosana, would serve as outposts, like that of Macpela for Abraham. This prediction was confirmed a few weeks later when it was learnt that the fourth and last evangelist, Asaele, had passed away. The costs for travel, exploration and settling the two missionaries and four evangelists, amounted to 50.000 Francs, ten of which would be underwritten by the Lesotho churches.

In conclusion, Coillard insisted on the responsibility of the churches in France: "Let me insist that, in this undertaking, the responsibility has to rest with the churches of France, and on you, gentlemen, who represent them. The Lesotho churches have gained in experience since their first enthusiastic response to the project. They have understood the importance and demands of the work, and are also aware of their weaknesses. They are not discouraged, but it is to you that they turn. They will follow, but don't ask them to pave the way."

During the discussion following on the report, the only objection was from Eugène Bersier. He felt the Paris Mission should start a new mission in the French colonies of Senegal or Indo-China rather than in an area under the influence of the British. But Pressensé cut the discussion short, reminding them that the new project in Zambezi could not be separated from the previous work in Lesotho which the Paris Mission had always expected to lead to further mission work. Although in a minority on the Board, it was known that there was support for this position outside. However, the proof of this had to come through the response of the French Protestant churches to the call of the Board.

Appia's position paper proposed that the Board should neither abandon the scheme nor support a new effort to the Nyaï. Finally, the Board fully agreed with Coillard's view and, on condition that he could find the human and financial resources necessary, decided that: "a new expedition would be sent to the Zambezi to explore the terrain with full powers to found a station on healthy and favourable ground in the immediate or more distant vicinity of the Barotsi valley."

Once the prime responsibility of the Zambezi Mission no longer rested with the churches of Lesotho and thus, for the time being, the Lesotho Mission could not be used as a model for the Zambezi, it seemed advisable to identify what might be the motivating factors for the churches of Europe, which Coillard was invited to visit, to support this new venture.

The missionary and his wife thus undertook a round of visits which took them, over two years (May 1880 – May 1882) to most areas of France, Switzerland, Great Britain, Holland, Belgium and Italy. The same round of visits had been undertaken thirty years before to pioneer the Lesotho Mission.

## B. Coillard: Missionary or explorer?

From the very first meeting the Coillards were astonished to discover what subjects interested their audiences. Edouard Favre, their biographer, summed it up this way: "Like it or not, in Europe, Coillard had the reputation of being an explorer. On several occasions, his listeners wanted to hear him talk about his adventures rather than about the mission. This was painful for him."

Board-member Alfred Boegner, who accompanied him to the meeting of the Paris Geographical Society on 21 April 1880, remarked that even in that scientific circle, the missionary underlined the Protestant angle. The geographer Henri Jaccottet noted: "Coillard made a great impression. He was never at a loss in this very secular milieu, before a curious and well-informed audience. The missionary neither concealed nor avoided the facts; his discrete presence was his way of affirming his faith and attracting new support for his work.

While on their speaking tours the Coillards received numerous official tributes and scientific distinctions. After Paris came London in January 1881, where the Portuguese ambassador officially welcomed the couple to thank them for having saved the life of Serpa Pinto two years earlier in the Zambezi. In Antwerp, in March 1882, Coillard received a medal from the Geographic Society and was made an honorary member; his wife was enthusiastically applauded and received a bouquet of flowers from the King of Belgium.

"All this", wrote Coillard to Eugène Casalis "did not add to our importance for ourselves. It is not us, but Africa, our Mission Society and our Protestantism that are honoured". One notices nevertheless the spread of a personality cult: "Ah, Monsieur, we thought you were taller," someone exclaimed one day (he was in truth quite short). He replied: "Seen from afar, all things gain stature. I'm very short, a small man, very small. The Master alone is great. He must increase and I decrease."

In the society circles of Paris, London or Geneva in which the Coillards were not particularly at ease, they encountered curiosity but not much eager interest. The missionary did not hesitate to challenge ministers and the upper classes. A smart woman who invited them to dinner said "Oh, Sir, you interested us so much last night at Mr.X. You will tell us more exciting things this evening, won't you?" At one of these dinners, where negative comments were made about the cost of the expedition, Mme Coillard replied: "I notice that on this table there is enough to pay for a good part of that expedition." Thus, with slightly sardonic humour and a gift of repartee, the Coillards dealt with these situations.

However, they were truly distressed to note that the churches tended to take the same demagogic approach. On 12 February 1882, Coillard wrote from Caen: "I preached this morning and we had our meeting in the evening; yet again a large audience. Right from the start I openly declared that I spoke as a missionary and not as an explorer. No one left the room, they listened patiently… except when the collection plate went round".

A few days later, Coillard was invited by the pastor of Mer (Loir et Cher) to speak to a non-religious audience which, according to him, included a considerable number of free thinkers. The pastor suggested that the meeting should not begin with prayer and a hymn, so as not to frighten away the public. He asked Coillard to tell lots of lion stories but at the same time, to slip in a spiritual note. So Coillard related his expedition in the Nyaï country, how his wagon got stuck and how his wife was threatened with death, how his helpers were trapped by aggressive warriors. Then, looking straight into the eyes of his audience he spoke out: "And you, what would you have done in my case?" No one answered and in the dead silence that followed Coillard said: "Well, I prayed and God answered me."

## C. An enthusiastic welcome but tepid support

In the church milieu, Coillard realised that there was little knowledge about the mission field and as a result, little interest. On 30 May 1881, he wrote to the Committee in Montpellier: "With few exceptions, our work seems to be on the same footing as charities to which little is donated and for which there is no sense of responsibility; it is less the work of the churches than of individual interest. It still meets with prejudice, and the same objections are made as 50 years ago. That's the dark side, but there are also rays of light." In Europe Coillard met with an enthusiastic public reaction to his exploits as a missionary explorer, but he was concerned that the Zambezi Mission was perceived as his own personal affair.

In Montpellier, he found himself half-way through his leave. The amount he needed for the expedition had been raised. Two free lay preachers had offered their services during the first meetings and were accepted by the Board. Frédéric Christol was an art teacher in Paris and M. Choquet was a teacher at Pouilly. Some friends urged him to set up the Zambezi Mission without delay. But he objected that the available funds would suffice to start it up but were insufficient for its continuation, so he spoke to the Board: "It is necessary at all costs to collect funds for the future. May I add that as long as the Board has not agreed with the colleagues in Lesotho, I would be very hesitant to take on the heavy responsibility of founding the Mission of the Zambezi."

On the advice of Mabille, who was in Paris, the Board on 13 June 1881 told Coillard that for the time being, they would not ask for help from the Church Conference of Lesotho, which was suffering the effects of the War of Guns. However, in view of the success of his Mission conferences, the Board would carry the responsibility for the work in the Zambezi.

Without doubt, the failure of the Lesotho Churches and the Conference due to the war put the Board in a difficult position and obliged it to present the Zambezi Mission as its own initiative. Yet Alfred Boegner, a few weeks earlier, had solemnly declared to the General Assembly of the Paris Mission that: "this Mission is not an arbitrary or isolated decision, the costly folly of a rich association that can, in order to renew public interest, afford such adventurous enterprises. It is the logical follow-up to the efforts made by Lesotho to found an outbound mission." Boegner, evidently, tried to dissociate the Mission to the Zambezi from the other successful expeditions of the time and to maintain its link to the Lesotho Mission. But as time went on, it became more and more difficult to maintain this argument. The three main reasons were:

-         The public taste for exotic adventure, even in church circles;
-         The nature of the projected mission which for the time being was nothing but an expedition;
-         The reservations expressed by Colliard's Lesotho colleagues.

On 21 December 1881, the Board was preoccupied by news from them: Paul-Amos Dormoy, Coillard's successor at Leribe, announced his early return to France for family reasons; Theophile Jousse explained his objections to the exploration programme, asking that Coillard return to Leribe and announcing his own return to France; Paul Germond wondered if the launch of the expedition under the current circumstances was appropriate; and Hermann Dieterlen asked to be informed of Coillard's plans.

Aware of all the confusing and problematic aspects of the Zambezi Mission, the Board on 21 December wondered if it should not purely and simply abandon the project. However, it rejected this possibility, decided the expedition should be undertaken and assured Coillard, its leader, of their moral support.

## D. The Zambezi: a heroic mission

The Board's final decision in favour of the expedition to the Zambezi ratified the fact that, from the start of Coillard's tours in Europe, a new model and a new mission strategy had come to the fore in the Paris Mission. Instead of transposing to the Zambezi the old Lesotho pattern and strategy of the churches exercising their apostolic mission, this would be an avant-garde project, with outside support, that would attempt to carry out a risky exploration into an unknown area of central Africa in the search for a new mission field. And leading this advance-party, a couple thrust onto the public scene by the press, likened to the greatest explorers of the time: Livingstone in whose footsteps they had trod and Serpa Punto who owed them his life.

A quick glance at the religious press coverage of the Coillard's conference tours illustrates this double process of hero-worship and popularity, of which Coillard and his wife were both subject and object. The only complete text of one of Coillard's speeches was found in the Journal religieux du canton de Neuchâtel on 22 and 29 May 1880. One can assume that he gave approximately the same type of address wherever he went.

A comment on this conference given in the Lutheran Church of Billettes in Paris, appeared in the Témoignage of 8 May 1880: "For an hour and a half the gallant missionary expounded on his expedition. He did this so simply that it was only when thinking it over that one realised the amount of energy and perseverance, of trust in God, of charity, required to accomplish this perilous journey without accident, and without conflict with the natives. The attention of the audience never flagged for a moment."

The Témoignage reporter's remarks reveal the quality of Coillard's public speaking: he recounted his adventures and preached at the same time. His main theme in relating events was the victory over the obstacles of nature, of man and mind. Coillard spoke without emphasis, letting the listener draw his own religious or cultural conclusions from what he heard. Coillard's qualities of energy, perseverance, charity and trust in God acknowledged by the reporter of Témoignage, according to the sociologist, L. Millet, characterise the hero: nobility, outgoing vitality, creative action and generous ardour. According to Millet, a hero is noble because he confidently overcomes all the obstacles. His exuberant vitality results from his psychic energy; his personal creative action consistently appeals to society; his generous fervour does not cut him off from others, to whom he shows sympathy and charity. Millet concludes: "The heroic life is glorious because it overcomes the temptations of excess, and never parodies the essential dimensions of heroism."

The lay public, intellectual or political, certainly recognised the character traits of a hero in Coillard. As for the religious and Protestant public in particular, it took the same view, as was shown in the debate in the Protestant press when the expedition left for the Zambezi. Paradoxically, the supporters of evangelisation in the French colonies, opposed to this expedition, nevertheless called Coillard a hero.

In the famous article in the Signal of 23 June 1883, referred to earlier, Eugène Réveillaud wrote: "Missionary work requires the prestige and stimulus of a certain type of heroism, of dangers to be met due to the climate and to men. From this point of view, the heroic aspect of the Lesotho Mission is over… That is why, whether he realises it or not, Mr Coillard, with the heart of a Christian hero – despite human wisdom and even Christian prudence – will blaze a new and different trail."

Coillard himself was surprised that in Protestant circles such a strange definition of heroism was given, and admitted in a letter to Georges Appia on 23 August 1883: "Worldly heroism may perhaps be a thirst for glory, but for me the heroism of a child of God means duty and obedience that the love of the Saviour of souls makes easy and joyful." Coillard, from now on, considered himself a simple soldier of Christ who obeys his orders.

Whatever idea Coillard might have had of the part he played in the public's perception of his role, one notices in his letters, systematically published in the JDME and more and more in the Protestant press, that he offered to the wider public, of which he was wary, and to the churches of Europe, of which he was so fond, new horizons that encouraged the former to dream and revived the hope of the latter, their pastors in particular.

From Italy, on 12 August 1881, he wrote to the Board and to mission friends: "In the towns and villages there are pastors who pursue their work without joy or blessing, in the strife and suffering of rival denominations that wither the soul, sharpen the spirit, and hide the royal banner under a cloud of dust. They are stifled and find no place in the sun; the framework in which they live is too narrow for their activities. And yet, beyond the seas we show to them a world where millions are perishing from lack of the Good News!"

Having come to the end of his tours and before leaving Europe for Africa, Coillard felt the urge to write a letter to the churches, reminding them of the objections to the mission he had encountered, to which he responded vigorously. To those who ceaselessly repeated: "What's the use of evangelising elsewhere when there is so much to be done locally", or "should we not rather evangelise the populations under French colonial domination rather than those under foreign domination or on the way to being so?" His reply was: "Why should we impose on the Kingdom of Jesus Christ the frontiers of our country or the limits of a district?" He added, for his colleagues: "When you, beloved and respected brethren, realise that the work of evangelisation in the world is not a luxury for the church which, if necessary, could be dispensed with, but a duty, a vocation, which the Master himself has entrusted to her, which she can neither ignore nor neglect with impunity, then you will know that your personal responsibility is directly involved, you will move your flocks and stir vocations among your young people."

However, after two years of touring in Europe, he had not won the theological support of his colleagues and not a single pastor had volunteered to accompany him to the Zambezi. He reminded them that by obliging him to speak to audiences he did not feel comfortable with they had morally compromised themselves vis-à-vis the public and, after having sponsored his appearances in this way, they should not forget the work he was to carry out far away from them in Africa. Coillard concluded somewhat wryly: "That will console me for what I have so often complained about, that the explorer was more popular then the missionary."

# III

# THE EXPEDITION AND FOUNDATION
# OF THE MISSION TO THE ZAMBEZI

## A. A year and a half of waiting and preparation in Lesotho (August 1882 – January 1884)

Coillard's complaints contrasted with the resolutely encouraging tones of Boegner at the General Assembly of the Paris Mission on 27 April 1882, during which he announced Coillard's departure the following day: "Currently, more than 100.000 francs have been put aside for the new mission. Thus, as far as financial resources are concerned, the response from the churches is beyond doubt; the same applies to the Mission workers." But the churches referred to were more from abroad than from France, from Switzerland in particular. Gifts and collections for the Zambezi Mission brought in more than 71.000 francs between 1881-1882, 50.000 of which came from abroad, mainly Switzerland.

As for the mission workers, a single man, Frédéric Christol, his wife and months-old baby accompanied Coillard and his wife. The other candidate, M. Choquet, withdrew in February 1882, following pressure from his parish at Pouilly and a petition from the Consistory of Bourges. It should be noted that these two lay workers had offered Coillard their services already at the outset of his speaking tours. Since then, not a single pastor, nor other Frenchman had volunteered for the Zambezi. Clearly, Protestant France did not feel concerned by the pressing appeals made by Coillard.

Among the other possible candidates, Dorwald Jeanmairet, a young Swiss watchmaker, who had become an evangelist in the Free Church of Neuchâtel joined Coillard in Lesotho, accompanied by Boegner in February 1883. Paul Maechling, a teacher from Montbeliard applied, but nothing came of it.

After Dormoy's resignation at Leribe, Jacques Weitzecker, a pastor from the Waldensian Church of Italy, working in Nice, responded to Coillard's call of August 1881. He took up his post in December 1883 at the time Christol's second child was born. On Coillard's advice, Christol decided not to go to the Zambezi and stayed at Hermon in Lesotho.

Finally, only two French people, Coillard and his niece Elise, started off on the expedition to the Zambezi on 2 January, 1884. Besides Dorwald Jeanmairet, the other participants were Christina Coillard, of Scottish origin, William Waddel, a Scottish cabinet-maker who had been recruited by Coillard a few months before in the Orange Free State and George Middleton, an Englishman living in Natal, also recruited by Coillard. There were also twelve Sothos of whom three were evangelists, Levi, Esaïe and Jonathan, a young Pedi, Philip, and two young Lozi, Seajika and Karumba, brought back by Coillard from his previous expedition, one of whom had stayed at Leribe, and the others at Morija, during his trip to Europe. The difficulties in making up the group and the civil war in Lesotho, in Leribe in particular, were the main reasons for this belated departure.

Coillard, who had probably expected that numerous young Frenchmen would join him after his trip to Europe, was very upset on hearing the criticism expressed by Auguste Mettetal and Eugène Réveillaud in the Protestant press about the activities of the Paris Mission in Southern Africa. On 6 January 1884, as the imposing caravan of four wagons each drawn by sixteen oxen set off on its way to Zambezi, Coillard wrote a letter to the mission friends in his inimitable style: "The freezing wind which has been blowing since I left France has, alas, withered in many hearts the confidence granted us and the interest surrounding our venture... It is hard on the soldiers who are ready for the assault and cannot turn back, to hear those who had encouraged them now say: "Go ahead ! but it's unlikely we shall follow..." Are you going to abandon us, friends of France, brothers and sisters from the Piedmont, from Switzerland, from Belgium, from Holland, from England and Scotland? No, you shall not, and before we reach the Zambezi you will once again give us tangible proof of your co-operation, of your heartfelt messages which touch our hearts, raise our courage, fortify our faith, and keep us going."

The caravan which reached the shores of the Zambezi in August 1884 was made the richer by the presence of Aaron, Andrew and their families, two Sotho evangelists picked up at Seleka, where they had been left six years earlier. However, Philip and Jonathan left the caravan, the first preferring to stay in his country and the second joining the Swiss Mission in Valdezia. But of new European fellow-workers, there were none.

## B. The end of the expedition and the founding of the Mission to the Zambezi (1885-1887)

After negotiating for a year with the Lozi chiefs, during which the expedition, stationed at Leshoma, suffered hunger and disease, discouragement and even the revolt of the Africans, Coillard received permission to cross the Zambezi at Kazungula on 19 August, 1885. Coillard wrote to the

Board: "Please do tell our friends that the strength and development of the mission depends entirely on their co-operation. Let them not wait for death to reduce our small staff."

Reinforcements arrived only two years later, the 20 August 1887. Coillard and Jeanmairet welcomed at Kazungula three new missionaries: Pastor Louis Jalla and his wife from the Italian Waldensian valleys, Henry Dardier, a doctor from Geneva and Auguste Goy, an agriculturalist from Vevey. With these new recruits, the Zambezi expedition was on its way. At François Coillard's request, the Paris Board on 5 December 1887 ratified this stage of the journey by a unanimous vote, officially adopting the Mission to the Zambezi as one of the projects it supported.

On reading the accounts of the first steps of the Zambezi Mission, it seems its foundation and development were based on the model of the Lesotho Mission. Jean-Paul Burger (President of the Mission 1927-1962) notes in his History of the Zambezi Church, that from the start, Coillard had had the vision of a people won over to the Gospel like the people of Lesotho, and had immediately identified the strategic points to be occupied, taking into consideration a sparsely populated country with fluvial communications.

A few days before he crossed the Zambezi, Coillard wrote to Casalis: "The Lesotho Mission was my education, of which I keep incomparable memories; the treasures of your first experiences laid the foundations on which we can build, even in the Zambezi."

The first meeting with King Lewanika (Robosi's new name on accession to the throne) on 23 March 1886 and the foundation of the Sefula station not far from Lealui, the capital, on 11 October 1887, were reminiscent of Casalis' first meeting with Moshoeshoe and the foundation of Morija (Lesotho) sixty years before. However, conditions were very different from those in Lesotho.

Coillard noted that the power of Lewanika, enthroned the year before at the price of frightful massacres, was still stained with his blood-thirsty methods. He could thus hardly compare this young chief to a new Moshoeshoe, though Lewanika aspired to resemble Khama, the Christian king of the Ngwatos, where he had taken refuge in 1885 and who had sent him messengers announcing Coillard's arrival. As for the Lozi social structures, they appeared to Coillard less developed than those of the Sothos and their customs cruder. Nevertheless, Coillard compared the two missions, keeping in mind the model, no doubt idealised, of the Lesotho Mission and its beginnings. Considering the different situations, two elements seemed to determine the continuation of the Mission:

- In Lesotho in 1833, the colonial power appeared to be far away and the independence of the Sotho was a fact. It was only ten years after their arrival that the French missionaries started to ask the British Government to guarantee the independence of the Sotho. In the Zambezi in 1886, Lewanika's first request to Coillard was to help him write a letter to Queen Victoria to request British protection to bolster his own power. We shall learn later the result of this request.

- The Lozi country was unhealthy, prey to a debilitating climate and to seasonal flooding of the river which fostered marshland, a perfect breeding ground for malaria-carrying mosquitoes, tse-tse flies and wild animals. None of these existed in Lesotho. The sanitary conditions and the morale of the Zambezi Mission members deteriorated rapidly.

At the beginning of 1887, the two Lozis of the expedition defected, accepting important positions at the King's court, although they were meant to be setting up an annexe near the capital. Then, in November 1887, it was Middleton's turn. Unable to live up to the exigencies of mission life and no doubt because of misunderstandings with Coillard, he decided to leave, although he had started making bricks to build permanent housing. He remained in the country, but was critical of the Mission's work.

As for the newcomers, their health rapidly deteriorated and death struck mercilessly. Dardier was the first to fall ill on the way from Sesheke to Sefula, a few days after his arrival. Sunstroke and malaria obliged him to return to Sesheke where the Jallas had been sent along with Dorwald Jeanmairet and Elise Coillard who had become his wife. Dardier was still able to assist the birth of Marguerite Jalla (13 January 1888). Then, against the advice of his colleagues, he left for Kazungula, obsessed by the idea of leaving the country, despite the fact that the area was overrun by one of Lewanika's rivals. Dardier, in a very weak condition, died on 23 February 1888.

Coillard wrote in his journal: "It will no doubt be seen as bad mark for the Zambezi, which had started to improve its image in the opinion of the Christian public. Will it quash the vocations of future mission doctors?" A month later Marguerite Jalla was carried away by fever, followed by Paballo Lefi on 4 August and two-year old Marguerite Jeanmairet, on 24 December. In August 1888, Coillard had to accept the return to Lesotho of Lefi and Aaron, the two evangelists, Lefi's wife being constantly ill and Aaron who found life too difficult in the Zambezi.

As a result, Coillard started to have doubts: "I have said and repeated it to others, I believed in it. If ever Africa is to be evangelised, it must be done by its own children. I counted on the Christian Basouto… were we misled? Were our theories, however beautiful, however seductive, but a dream which is now fading?" However, he rapidly countered these questions by asserting: "The spirit of God is upon the churches of Lesotho and, as we know, there, as in France and everywhere, the spirit of life is the missionary spirit." He already saw this assertion being applied in practice since all the Lozi chiefs without exception appeared to be favourably disposed to sending their sons and nephews to the mission schools. Two were already functioning with some fifty pupils; one in Sefula since March 1887, including Lewanika's son Litia, and the other in Sesheke since end-1887. But to continue this effort, Coillard noted, one had to have 'elite, competent staff'.

It happened that at the same time, the Mission to the Congo had started up. In early 1888, the Paris Mission was able to send three teachers and an artisan; two were French and two were Swiss. Coillard did not agree with those who feared that the Zambezi might be sacrificed to the Congo Mission. And, more convinced than ever, he wrote: "The demonstration of its essential, catholic and universal character must be taken to heart. Far above the prejudices, interests and flags of their respective nations, Christians must raise the banner of the cross. And we, the sons of Huguenot Protestants, French at heart, who have taken the initiative of this great work, in a country where we answer to no European power, are we putting France to shame? Shall we renounce our country…or will it renounce us?" Alas, this Huguenot France called on by Coillard from the shores of the Zambezi would not join him for quite some time.

## C. Was the heroic mission on the way to becoming a martyrdom? 1889-1892: the terrible years

In 1893, as Coillard entered his 60th year and was feeling the weight of material and moral difficulties, he wrote to Boegner on 23 July: "I am talking about the possibility that after my death the Zambezi Mission will cease to be a French mission and will pass into other hands … As far as I am concerned, national interests are extraneous and should not be taken into consideration. But while working in the Zambezi as a child of, and a representative of, the churches of my country, I always believed I was working for their good. But if the Zambezi Mission is too heavy a load for the faith of our friends in France, why not tell us so frankly?" Indeed, after seven years of labour, not one French missionary had come forward.

Nevertheless, two new stations were opened, each with a school, one in Kazungula, the gateway to the country, in October 1889, then in Lealui, a central point near the capital in October 1892. In Coillard's mind, these two posts completed the chain of stations on the model of Lesotho which, against all odds, Coillard wanted to build along the Zambezi. But was this not over-ambitious, in view of the available resources? According to the 1892 Conference report, at least one missionary and one evangelist were needed for each station. This proved to be impossible in view of the losses among the mission staff. The arrival of three missionaries, Adolphe Jalla from Italy, Elise Kiener from Switzerland and Emile Vollet from Alsace was no compensation for the premature departures and desertions.

Ten months after his arrival, Adolphe Jalla left to get married and only returned two years later. The Jeanmairet couple left in 1890 for health reasons and continued work in Lesotho. Emile Vollet left in 1892 after disagreement with his colleagues and went to work in Lesotho. André, the pioneer evangelist and Mwanangombe, the first Lozi to be baptised (May 1890) moved into Lewanika's service in 1892.

The mission families continued to suffer bereavement; three children died (Anita Jalla in 1890 and, in 1891 Emile Goy and a still-born child in Kanedi's family, the Sotho evangelist brought by Vollet), and Christina Coillard and Kanedi's wife Josephina died in October 1891.

The Jalla brothers (Louis and Adolphe) had insisted that, in such unhealthy conditions, where the missionary had to put such physical energy into building a house, where communications were difficult and the population spread out, it would be better to concentrate their energies on two main points in the Zambezi valley. There they could then train evangelists to go out into the country. However, this solution was not taken into consideration. Without doubt this is one of the reasons which prevented the development of the Zambezi Mission and led its personnel, particularly the locals, to abandon the mission.

It is interesting that Maurice Leenhardt (a Paris missionary from the Pacific) who visited the Zambezi Mission in 1923, noted that forty years after its foundation the persistent idea of a chain of stations had paradoxically limited its actions in three respects: for the locals "Little training in responsibility, a lack of trust, too heavy a load on the missionary". In terms of training: "education which was too scholastic; no religious or biblical component and insufficient space for the church. As for the missionary, not enough field work and narrow limits on activities and, vis-à-vis the locals, a lack of trust, the limits of which barred the work of the spirit."

Another factor in the loss of confidence in the Zambezi Mission was the question of the British Protectorate granted to Lewanika in June 1890 in which Coillard was compromised. It is necessary to relate this important episode in the history of the Mission in order to try to understand the part played by Coillard in the transfer of the Lozi country to British control.

## D. The question of the British Protectorate

We have already mentioned that, on his arrival in Sefula in October 1886, Lewanika asked Coillard to help him approach Queen Victoria to request her protection, in the same way as his friend Khama had done. Khama, in accord with the London Mission Society, had written to Victoria and obtained in 1884 a British Protectorate over his possessions. This had granted him safety from his rivals, the Ndebele of Lobengula and the Boers. Coillard, who did not want to compromise his religious mission work by taking a premature political position, refused to write to the Queen. He advised Lewanika to first ask the advice of Khama, whose situation was not as secure as Lewanika pretended. British sovereignty was represented by a commercial company whose views were, according to him, closer to those of the Cape government than to those of London. But Lewanika repeated his request on several occasions and, confronted with the continued refusal of Coillard, created a surprise by calling a people's assembly in October 1888 to try to sanction the idea that if Khama had missionaries and soldiers, Lewanika should have them too.

After a long and troubled debate, people looked to Coillard who declared: "As servants of God, we have absolutely nothing to do with soldiers or with the British government, nor with any other government." He reported that: "I insisted and made it clear. I added that being totally impartial on the question as I was French, I was willing if absolutely necessary to help with my advice and support them in their negotiations. I concluded by explaining what a protectorate was, its implications, etc."

After several discussions which displeased Lewanika, since none of them included stationing soldiers in the country (they would, in fact, have been used to eliminate his opponents), Coillard concluded that the majority had understood and trusted him. So, in January 1889, he agreed to write a letter to the British Governor of Botswana (Bechuanaland), Sir Sidney Sheppard, to solicit British protection. To this letter was added another from Lewanika to Khama asking for his opinion.

On 17 July 1889, Khama replied that he had every reason to be satisfied with the situation, as the nation of the Great Queen was with him and that he lived peacefully with them. He feared neither the Ndebele nor the Boers who for a long time had not attacked him. He would even be able introduce him to an envoy of the British Government. On 1 September 1889, it was Sheppard's turn to reply to Coillard. As explained by C.W. Mackintosh, he was informed that Mr Rhodes had written to the British South Africa Company to support Lewanika. Without knowing the background, the BSA jumped at the opportunity. Very soon after, the envoy, Mr Elliot Lochner, left for Barotseland to start negotiations. But it was a bad time of year for travelling and he arrived only in April 1890. Concurrently, Cecil Rhodes wrote to Coillard asking him if, momentarily, he could not himself take over the office of Resident of the Company in the country.

Although he had welcomed Lochner, ill and destitute, in his home, and the negotiations with Lewanika had not yet started, Coillard replied to Rhodes on 4 April 1890: "I am slightly doubtful of Mr. Lochner's mission…You ask me to take over the Residency. I cannot serve two masters. But if, without having an official title, and until you find the right man, I can be of some help to your company as a medium of communication [sic], I willingly put myself at your disposal." Obviously Coillard took enormous risks committing himself so deeply in political questions. Did he realise what he was doing? No doubt he did not, but one can safely say that in offering himself as a 'medium of communication' between the foreigners and the locals, he believed in good faith that he was defending the best interests of both sides with, however, a sincere but naïve confidence in the civilising role of Great Britain…

In fact Coillard was a worthy apostle engaged in spite of himself in an international conflict that lay beyond his control: a few years earlier, he had welcomed and saved the Portuguese explorer Serpa Pinto with the same generosity he was now giving the British envoy Lochner, who had arrived in tatters. Britain and Portugal had in the meantime become rivals for power between the Kololos and the Ndebele along the lower reaches of the Zambezi.

Finally, on 27 June 1890, a treaty between Lochner and Lewanika was signed, witnessed by Coillard, putting the Lozi country under British control. But it further poisoned Anglo-Portuguese relationships concerning the boundaries of Lake Nyasa. The international convention of 20 August 1890, in the spirit of the Berlin Act, by which the boundaries of the future Mozambique and Rhodesian colonies were fixed, finally settled things.

Hardly had the Lochner Treaty been signed, but the worst accusations poured down on Coillard from all sides: he had sold the country to foreigners. This accusation came from Middleton, a former field worker of the Mission who had returned to Lealui on 21 October 1890 in the king's service. "He came with two other Europeans", recounts Jean-Paul Burger, "with the aim of gaining mining rights for a company in Kimberley, but alas it was too late. Irritated by this failure, Middleton started a campaign disparaging the chartered company and the Mission, accusing them of having deceived Lewanika and his chiefs. He repeatedly said the king had not obtained the protectorate but had simply sold the country to a commercial company that would leave him nothing."

Lewanika summoned Coillard to Lealui to account for his actions in the presence of Middleton. The summons were expressed in such disrespectful terms that Coillard refused to go. An angry correspondence between Coillard and the king ensued but, on seeing that the Sesheke chiefs and queen Mokwaye of Nalolo were taking Middleton's part, Coillard consented to go to Lealui on 29 May 1891.

Coillard's position was very awkward: "We talked over the nature of the company," wrote Coillard in his journal. "I enhanced it, whereas Middleton reduced it to the rank of a simple mining company. The weak point in my argument, which alas I recognise, is that the contract with that company is made in the light of a contract or an alliance with the Queen's government and not by the government itself. The alliance is inferred in the contract, it affirms it and it will be carried out without delay just as the British East Africa Company has done." On the day of this angry meeting, the BSA was no longer the commercial and mining company founded by Rhodes to federate the different British establishments in Southern Africa. In October 1889, it had obtained a royal charter which gave it the rights of British sovereignty over a vast territory situated between Botswana (Bechunanaland) and Zambia (Barotseland or Zambezi). This covered internal security, international treaties, commercial monopoly, money, abolition of slavery, etc.

Coillard was thus in a strong position to defend Lochner's treaty and Middleton could justly bring forward his own business concerns. But, according to Coillard, Middleton was defending his own interests while pretending to be 'the champion of the natives', while Coillard was defending the interests of the Lozi nation which Britain alone was able to protect.

To get out of this dilemma, Coillard suggested that Lewanika send a message to the BSA stating that, in signing with Lochner, what he and the king wanted was essentially the protectorate of Great Britain. After much hesitation the king accepted. In this message of 1 January 1891, Coillard informed the representative of the company in Botswana that as his efforts on their behalf had been compromised by doubts about his honesty, and his position as a disciple of Jesus Christ had become untenable, he was withdrawing from all political affairs.

In November 1891, Coillard heard in a letter from H. Loch, the governor of the Cape, dated 11 September, that Queen Victoria recognised the treaty between Lewanika and the BSA and that she had nominated Harry Johnston, a well-known explorer, to settle in the Lozi country as soon as possible. "That's exactly what was needed to disperse our political fogs", wrote Coillard to the Board on 11 November.

In fact, the British resident only arrived in October 1897, after the BSA had managed to eliminate its chief opponent, the Ndebele chief Lobengula who, right up to his death in 1894, had organised resistance against British concessions. When Major Coryndon arrived, Adolphe Jalla had once more to explain the situation to Lewanika, who didn't believe that the major was coming to the capital as the Queen's representative. Was he not perhaps sent by the BSA which was so unpopular with the African nationalists? As for Middleton, who had fallen from favour after the recognition of the Lochner Treaty, he left the country in 1892, never to return.

The causes of this critical two-year period which explain the exhaustion of the Coillards and perhaps Christina's death, were unknown to the Board and mission friends. Coillard's involvement since 1889 in obtaining the British Protectorate was never mentioned either in private or official correspondence. From 1889-1892, readers of the JDME were informed of international political affairs and of the British Protectorate of the Lozi country only thanks to the reports of Frédéric-Hermann Krüger. On several occasions, however, Coillard did mention political agitation concerning Lewanika's concessions, first to the Ware Company in Kimberley in June 1889 and then to Lochner and the BSA in April 1890. At that time he mentioned that he was being accused by the king of having sold part of the country and was preparing to sell the rest. But he never explained why and Middleton's name was never mentioned.

His conclusion about the signature of the Lochner treaty, published in the JDME in December 1890, was that, "for the moment I must abstain from all comment," though he added, "I have no doubt whatever that this is the only solution for this nation… to raise a permanent barrier against the invaders, the immigrants and gold diggers." These letters to the Mission House raised no debate whatever, as the Board was preoccupied elsewhere with the Girard affaire in Tahiti and by the forthcoming voyage of Boegner to Senegal. They seemed in general sympathetic about the trials suffered by the missionaries and to respond to the most urgent need – to send reinforcements...

One might with reason wonder why Coillard did not inform the Board of his diplomatic activities. Had he done so, one would have understood that in the nationalistic context of the time, the Board might not have let the Mission friends know. In fact, the Committee knew nothing at all because, since Coillard's return to the Zambezi, not a single traveller nor missionary had returned to France to report in person on what had happened there. The assumption is that Coillard earnestly believed that after three years of testing Lewanika's goodwill, he could, without consulting the Board, justify his claim for the Protectorate. Was it not in the missionary tradition of people like Moffat and Casalis, whose work he venerated, to be the king's adviser? Then, when Coillard realised that protection from a European power in 1885 was not applied as it had been 40 years earlier, he tried to take upon himself the sole consequences of his acts, to the point of martyrdom. He did this so as not to compromise the Board of the Paris Mission which was at the time in great difficulties over Senegal, Tahiti and Madagascar. When at last the political horizon cleared with the recognition of Lochner's British treaty, Coillard was free to confirm, in the pathetic letter announcing the death of his wife, that all the slander and calumny he had suffered were now reduced to nothing.

Christina Coillard's death meant that the months of moral torture were buried with her and gave renewed strength to her survivor. Boegner wrote in February 1892 that: "it seems François Coillard's desire to devote himself to his work has never been greater." He cited Coillard: "She has finished her work, but I have not finished mine. I shall find strength in my God. I shall rise up and I shall work again. I shall live for this Mission that the Lord called us to build together on the Zambezi".

# IV

# THE SECOND FOUNDING OF THE CHURCH OF ZAMBEZI

Following the visit of James Johnston, a Scottish missionary, on December 5 1892, the Paris Mission Board slowly shed its uncritical admiration of the Zambezi Mission and gradually became aware of the actual facts. Johnston was a missionary in Jamaica; he had just returned from a voyage to Africa with six black Jamaicans, whom he had enabled to discover their roots. He had crossed central Africa in the steps of Livingstone and spent several weeks with Coillard who had taken him to visit the mission stations. Speaking to the Board, he drew a flattering picture of the Zambezi Mission, underlining what a great honour it was for French Protestantism to have the only Christian mission in such a vast region. But he drew their attention to the very difficult conditions of work of the missionaries, to Coillard's very poor health, (incidentally, he advised Coillard not to settle in Lealui) and said that if the Paris Mission wanted to keep him, reinforcements should be sent.

## A. Coillard's forced return to Europe

As a result of the meeting with James Johnston, the Board decided to create a special commission to deal specifically with the affairs of Lesotho and the Zambezi. On 16 June 1893, at its first meeting, the Commission confirmed that Edgar Kruger, an Alsatian missionary artisan who had left for the Zambezi to take Waddell's place (while on leave), had had to stay in Lesotho. Since Kruger was on his way to help Coillard settle in Lealui, the Commission took advantage of this mishap to ask Coillard not to found the new station and, instead, to plan a trip to Europe which seemed necessary for his health and in the interest of the mission's work.

When on 17 November Coillard received the Committee's instructions, he had already been settled in Lealui for a year. The faithful Waddell had postponed his leave to oversee the gigantic work of building the station with the help of about a hundred men (construction of a bridge, a church and two small cabins). On learning that Eugène Béguin, a Swiss pastor and his wife, were soon to be sent out, Coillard did not see that it was necessary to return to Europe. In his journal, he wrote: "Leave, when you are 60! The thought of lecturing in Europe terrifies me. But I am ready for anything. If only I could stay another five years here! But God knows..."

By end-November 1893, the Committee learnt from reliable sources that the state of Coillard's health was alarming. It remembered what Johnston had told them the year before and decided to formally advise and pressure Coillard to return to Europe to recover his health, thinking that in France he could best serve the cause to which he was dedicated. Normally, such a call was an imperative and the Committee would not waive the principle concerning the leave of missionaries. Coillard had the right to it and was to obey. But his answer was no. His letter of 27 April 1894 is subtly worded. While recognising the solemn nature of the Committee's call, he declared he had put the question before God and was unable to discern whether he was indeed called to Europe. His duty was therefore to remain where he was posted, mainly because:

-       His health had improved and was better than that of all the other missionaries.
-       The hoped-for reinforcements not having arrived, to leave now would be desertion and would leave too heavy a burden on his colleagues.
-       A trip to Europe at sixty would leave him little hope of returning to Africa. Yet it was there, and there only, alongside his wife's grave, that he saw his future.

Faced with such arguments, the Committee was speechless and on 8 October 1894, Boegner decided to publish Coillard's letter 'in extenso' in the JDME of November 1894, which no one objected to.

The Board's unusual attitude towards Coillard is somewhat surprising. Did it imply that he who had gone it alone, against the will of the majority, having taken little account of the Committee's calls for prudence, held a place apart in the missionary body, a sort of shareholder above the law? No doubt, but what was understandable when Coillard was an explorer, seemed less so once the mission was founded. Should there have been another strategy?

It seems the reason for this apparently passive attitude of the Committee when faced with Coillard corresponds to the spirit of the times, typified by Boegner and several other members of the Committee, including Georges Appia. One should remember that this was a period of colonial conquest; in France in particular, where the Ministry of Colonies was created in 1894, the problem of Madagascar predominated in people's minds. Christian missions were considered to be part of the conquest, peaceful perhaps but with a triumphant vocabulary and a practice of territorial occupation whose main slogan was reinforcement and support. A single example illustrates this fact: in his editorial in the JDME of

November 1894 entitled 'Our Aim', Boegner indicates that the history of
the beginnings of the Zambezi Mission recalled the conquest of Algeria
by French soldiers! "In both cases a handful of men were able, through
miracles of patience, energy and activity, not only to maintain themselves
in enemy territory, but to set up outposts, establish strong positions, lay
siege and conquer fortresses. But if our missionaries, while accomplish-
ing their work with the help of God, did their duty, it is for us to do ours
by helping in doubling or tripling their number so as to make their victo-
ries final for the Church which expects it. Let us make an effort, says M.
Coillard in a special letter in July 1894, that we may find ten dedicated
missionaries and twice the number of evangelists within two or three
years."

As far as Boegner was concerned, one may add that the Zambezi
Mission was for him an apostolic work in its purest form; it penetrated
into places where the Gospel had never been heard of, it did not follow
the behest of French nationalism and, for the time being, it was tied neither to an important scholastic or social institution nor even to a church
charity. It was a unique case in the work of the Paris Mission. Even the
most recent venture in Gabon was starting to give Boegner worrying
signs due to the tendency of the missionaries to develop scholastic and
industrial branches of their work. Boegner's convictions were confirmed
by John Mott's movement of voluntary students for mission whose motto
was: "Make Christ King in this generation". This work among laymen
and students was intended to raise an army composed of an advance party
of missionaries and a rearguard of mission friends.

So, in the end, despite the rules, it fell to Coillard, and possibly the
Zambezi Conference, to decide on the most convenient time for him to go
to Europe. In these conditions, it could be expected that Coillard would
be at death's door before he considered returning to Europe.

During the Lealui Conference (13-24 September 1895), Coillard suffered an acute kidney infection, which forced him to conduct the debates
from his bed. He then agreed to go to Kimberley to consult a doctor,
accompanied by Mr and Mrs Louis Jalla who were returning to Europe
on leave, and two Lozis, Samata and Stephen Semondji, a boy very close
to Coillard. From there he planned a visit to Lesotho in order to stimulate
the churches' enthusiasm in favour of the Zambezi. He would then decide
whether a trip to Europe would be possible.

Coillard left Lealui carried on a stretcher on 30 October. He arrived in
Kimberley six months later travelling by wagon and by train and successfully survived an operation. But he was too weak to travel to Lesotho and

on 21 May 1896, after having undergone "the terrible temptation to turn back and return to the Zambezi", he embarked for England with his two Lozi companions and arrived on 11 June 1896.

On leaving Africa, Coillard felt that the Zambezi Mission had at last taken root: a fifth station had been founded by Eugène Béguin in Nalolo, the residence of Queen Mokwae, in October 1894. A Bible school had opened at Lealui in November 1894; when he left it was attended by eleven pupils. The Lealui Conference in September 1895 had welcomed five new arrivals: Pastor Emile Boiteux and his wife from Neuchâtel were posted to Kazungula, Paolo Davit from the Waldensian Valleys at Sefula, together with Sotho evangelists brought by the missionaries, Theodoro Pheko and Arone Njelapa, stationed at Lealui and Sesheke. A Swiss missionary artisan, Ivan Mercier, was expected to open a trade school at Sefula.

But this edifice was very fragile as it depended on people from outside: the European missionaries and the Sotho evangelists whose understanding of the country was limited and whose health was constantly failing. What is more, during Coillard's journey to Lesotho, Auguste Goy died on 26 April 1896 and the series continued with the death in December of the Sotho evangelist Theodore Piso and in March 1897, of his son Eugène to be followed by Giulio, Adolph Jalla's first son.

It is noteworthy that, ten years after the founding of the Mission, there was still not officially a Church of the Zambezi. The only baptised person, Mwanangombe, having gone over to Lewanika's service, had left the country. In one way, this situation is to the credit of the missionaries who never enforced conversions; they followed the Lesotho discipline which required the renunciation of polygamy and other cultural practices before admission to baptism and communion. This implies that over 10 years, only one Lozi had been deemed worthy of entering the church...

Noting the wariness among the missionaries about the validity of a run of conversions in all their stations in 1894, Jean-Paul Burger (mission president 1927-1963) wondered if the mission: "had not involuntarily broken the momentum through a lack of confidence in the believers on the one hand, and by lack of faith in the power of the Holy Spirit on the other." Reflecting on Maurice Leenhardt's theory concerning the sombre outlook of the missionaries at the time, Burger thinks that the demands made on believers caused much discouragement in the first generations of Africans brought into contact with the Christian faith.

## B. Coillard's second visit to Europe (1896-1898)

The founder of the Zambezi Mission who set foot in Southampton, despite all the reverses suffered, was typical of the tradition of mission-ary conquest, led by a body of elite foreigners, amongst whom he was the first soldier. As in 1880, he had come to Europe to recruit. Having heard, on arrival in Britain, of the death of Goy, he wrote on 15 July to Boegner: "Alas, our family circle in Zambezi was so small, and now we have another gap! So it is no longer ten but eleven workers we now need, not counting doctors and craftsmen."

A few weeks later, from his convalescence in Contrexéville, he raised the number to 15 and prepared a lecture tour of the churches of Europe to plead for the cause of the Zambezi Mission. However, in agreement with the Board, he decided the tour would only start in January 1897; until then he would work on a book on the beginnings of the Zambezi Mission, while touring Alsace, Switzerland and Italy.

It should be remembered that Coillard arrived when the Paris Mission Society was going through a difficult time. Henri Lauga and Frédéric H. Krüger, the French delegates sent to Madagascar, were on the point of returning to France; a controversy was raging in the press concerning their pro-English attitude which had a negative effect on the Society in general. In this context, an appeal to recruit 15 people for a country under British control could hardly be opportune.

Without doubt, the Madagascar question cast a shadow on the Zambezi. For example, Gustave Mondain, a young, recently-qualified arts and science teacher, had felt the call to follow Coillard at his first public appearance at l'Oratoire du Louvre in Paris on May 28, but the Board decided to allocate him to Madagascar: "His wish was to be a mis-sionary in the full sense of the word. However, he understood that his qualifications directed him to teaching, so he accepted to go to Madagascar", said the report of 23 November 1896.

On the whole, the craze to evangelise the French colonies forced the Board and Coillard to turn to a more discreet and personalised form of recruitment. Once again, the majority of candidates were to be found in countries other than France. But Coillard was not satisfied with that situ-ation. From Torre-Pellice where, on 10 December 1897, Coillard attend-ed the ordination of Auguste Coïsson, due to leave for the Zambezi, he wrote: "I have an uneasy feeling… a certain envy on behalf of the church-es of my country harasses me. In 1881, when I first visited these valleys, people were but little interested in mission… Since then, these churches, which are not rich, have sent nine of their sons and daughters to the mission. Seven of them went to the Zambezi. As for France, one single person; your servant..."

In October, in London, Coillard met an English evangelist, Alfred Mann and in March 1897, in St-Jean-du-Gard, a French artisan, Théophile Verdier, offered his services. Finally, in May, a Swiss pupil of the Mission school, Théophile Burnier, applied for the Zambezi. All three were accepted by the Board and left for the Zambezi in 1898. Verdier was thus the first Frenchman, but the Frenchman Coillard was hoping above all to find would be an ordained pastor who could, when the time came, take his place at the head of the Mission.

On 3 May 1897, Coillard presented his plan to the Board. He told them of the encouragement he had received throughout the country and notably at the Faculty of Theology of Montauban where missionary vocations seemed to be developing. He insisted on the need for several French missionaries to be found so that the leadership of the Zambezi Mission not be taken ever by others and that the bonds with the other branches of the Society not be broken, and so that the interest of the churches of France for this field be maintained.

He pleaded that the chain of mission stations be completed and to the objection: "Should one not reinforce the existing stations before considering their extension?" Coillard answered that both actions should go together: "The taking over of those parts of the country not yet evangelised was, by nature, the responsibility of our Society." The Board listened, promised to take into account the missionaries' requests, but could not make any decision, as minds were totally focused on management of the Madagascar crisis.

Then, on 10 June came the news of the assassination of Escande and Minault. On 14 June, the Board met to deal with this drama and had no time to attend to matters concerning the Zambezi. At the end of the meeting, they decided nevertheless to give a positive answer to Coillard's letter of 13 May asking that some of the theology student candidates from Montauban be assigned to the Zambezi. Finally, it was only on 8 November 1897 that this mission field appeared again on the agenda of the Board. Coillard and Louis Jalla had insisted in a letter that the candidates be sent out rapidly. Auguste Coïsson and Ivan Mercier had been held up by cattle fever and had not reached their destination. The Board decided therefore to send to the Zambezi one of the Montauban theology student candidates, Daniel Couve, scion of an important Bordeaux Reformed family and nephew of Benjamin Couve, member of the Board. This decision, they insisted prudently, should not be announced to the churches until the requests of the other mission fields had been reviewed and decided upon.

Alfred Boegner strongly recommended this candidate: "the aptitude and vocation of this young brother," he declared, "will carry him forward. Thanks to his gifted and enthusiastic nature and the circumstances in which his vocation was nurtured, he represents the general and apostolic aspects of our work." Indeed, Daniel Couve was the secretary of the Franco-Swiss student movement for mission. Together with a few of his Montauban theology faculty colleagues, he was instrumental in launching the first issue of the Almanach des Missions Evangéliques with a print-run of 7000, designed to popularise mission and support the work of the Paris Mission. It was destined to be a successful publication. The following year, twice that number was printed and it was published right up to the eve of the second world war. The editorial of the last number in 1937 entitled 'He must reign' was signed by Daniel Couve, by then director of the Paris Mission.

Not all agreed with Boegner, both within and outside the Board. Henri Lauga, who passed through Montauban after Coillard, informed the Board that he would prefer to see Couve in Madagascar; Pastor Gout, a member of the Board absent at the time of the unanimous vote to send Couve to the Zambezi, agreed. But their main concern was the opposition of the candidate's mother. She would have preferred her son to be sent to a colonial mission, preferably the Congo. Boegner corresponded with her in the hopes of changing her mind.

Coillard was evidently delighted by the decision: "I can well imagine the faith, love and steadfastness needed to take such a decision", he wrote to the Board on 21 November 1897 and, in his usual way, added: "you could hardly have done less. I might add, at the risk of seeming indiscreet, that more should be done... we must urgently and vigorously strengthen the French presence in Lesotho as well as the Zambezi... As you have said, and are now confirming by strengthening our ranks: we shall hold on! It is a pledge which enables us to add to our number and to expand our action."

But Coillard would very rapidly change his tune. First of all, he felt matters were being delayed as the Board focused on the Madagascar question. He inundated it with letters, insisting on the number of 15 missionaries. As for the expeditions, the one with Louis Jalla in 1898 (consisting of his wife, of Eugénie Specht, a teacher from Mulhouse, Alsace, whom Coillard had recruited in November 1897, Alfred Mann and his wife, and Georges Mercier, Ivan's brother, a Swiss artisan) and the one he intended to lead himself in the spring of 1899, would cost 150.000 francs he announced. On 8 July 1898, the Finance committee instructed Coillard not to exceed the 130.000 francs allocated to the Zambezi Mission", and to find the additional amount himself.

As for the Commission on Lesotho and the Zambezi which met a few days later, it continued to criticise the policy of the Zambezi Mission: it considered that it had not been firmly led, that it depended too much on Coillard, that the stations were too far apart, that they had too exclusively focused on Lewanika's court and family, that the Mission had no deep roots among the people, etc. It proposed to the Board that the number of missionaries to be sent out should be limited to seven, over and above the four already with Louis Jalla.

While recognising the 'boundless blessings' which the Mission and the Churches of Europe had received because of Coillard's speaking tours, the commission requested that Jean Bianquis, who six months earlier had joined the Board of Directors and became Director of the Paris Mission on Alfred Boegner's departure on 23 June for Madagascar, communicate these remarks to Coillard. Without doubt, Coillard lost in Boegner his most loyal supporter. But Bianquis had until then shown no opposition to the Zambezi Mission. However, though somewhat lacking in experience, he dealt with the situation with the firmness necessary to cope with Coillard's overwhelming demands. From then on, correspondence between the two became strained: Coillard felt that the Zambezi Commission's decision stifled people's vocations, and he refused to discuss the evaluation of his strategy towards the royal court. With just a few months left before his departure, he felt constrained to continue his speaking engagements, turning himself into a fund-raiser, which he loathed.

Bianquis then consented to send out an appeal from Coillard to the friends of the Zambezi Mission in Switzerland, Holland, Belgium, Italy and England, in a desperate last attempt to reach his goal in the three months left to him. This final appeal took up 10 pages in the JDME in September 1898.

A more serious difficulty awaited Bianquis. Since 1897, Coillard, through his speaking tours with captain Alfred Bertrand, had more or less achieved his aim of recruiting 15 missionaries, to be led by Daniel Couve. But then Couve's mother dropped a bombshell: through her eldest son Louis, she informed the Board that she and her family formally opposed the departure of her youngest son for the Zambezi. On 3 October 1898 the Board, "taking into consideration the gravity of the reasons given", had no choice but to accede to the request. While deeply regretting that circumstances forced it to deprive Coillard of the French missionary on whom he depended, the Board assigned Daniel Couve to the Congo and pledged to find a French pastor to take his place for the Zambezi.

One can imagine Coillard's reaction to this news: first of all, pain for the Zambezi Mission, "yet again in a destitute condition, yet again on the verge of getting qualified collaborators, and at the last moment it turns out to be but a mirage." It was also painful because Coillard had wanted the Zambezi Mission "to be the crowning glory of the churches of France." There was also the troubling feeling that the focus of mission was moving from France to other countries of Europe, certainly as far as the Zambezi was concerned and that, for French Protestantism, the focus was on colonial areas. Finally, he could not understand how the Board, when a young man had received a call, could give in to the demands of his family: "You cannot negotiate or do a deal with families; a vocation is a personal thing", wrote Coillard in a fury from London.

Ultimately, Coillard was proved partly right. At the Executive Committee meeting on 12 October 1898, Louis Sautter quoted a letter from Daniel Couve indicating that the Board's decision was not in keeping with his own personal wishes and those of his future wife, Inès Leenhardt, the daughter of a Montpellier doctor... Sautter was asked to write a note in the JDME explaining the reasons for the change in Couve's destination, and the candidate's personal position.

The Board recorded Coillard's criticism while considering that he had not weighed the impact of the situation it was faced with. It asked Georges Appia to write him a letter to restore the confidence between the Board and the missionary. It assured him that in Couve's change of posting, he should see neither a diminution of interest, nor of neglect for the work in Zambezi. Appia was able to announce to Coillard that the Board had called Jacques Liénard, a Montauban theology student, to take Couve's place. On the condition that the Faculty and the Ministry would agree to shorten the length of his studies, he agreed to volunteer.

But Coillard was resentful. He was impatient to return to the Zambezi and had already booked passage on a boat bound for South Africa, sailing from Southampton on 10 December 1898. He welcomed Liénard's application but left the Board to deal with the Faculty and the Government. He also thought it useless to organise a great public send-off in Paris.

Coillard's feelings improved on learning that the count of 15 people had been achieved and that funds for the expedition were almost on target. On 20 November 1898, he bid farewell to the Parisian public at a packed service at the Oratory. The ovations accompanied the Zambezi veteran and his companion Semondji all the way to the station platform on 23 November 1898. Everyone had in mind St Paul's words when leaving Miletus, Acts 20:25: "And now I know that none of you, among whom I have gone about proclaiming the kingdom, will ever see my face again."

## C. What was Coillard's secret?
When one considers that in June 1896 Coillard was brought home at death's door, that after two and a half years of tireless speaking engagements he had recruited a squad of 15 people and had himself raised the funds for the expedition, one cannot help wondering how he did it. He got no help from the Paris Mission. Yet, while Coillard was running around Europe, the Paris Mission recruited 54 people and raised 400.000 Francs for Madagascar. Factors that explain his achievements include:

### Coillard's personality
All the biographies and press cuttings on Coillard's conferences reveal his charismatic personality. His high profile in the press during his 1880-1882 visit has already been noted. Since then, Coillard's place in the hearts of Mission supporters had grown continually. No other mission tour had excited so much attention nor so many requests from local churches for his presence. When he appeared on the scene, it was like a dream come true. He fascinated his audience, all audiences, from children to intellectuals, from bourgeois to workmen and farmers. He had a talent for story telling; at every meeting he used illustrations drawn from his own photographs.

Edouard Favre notes that Coillard continually felt he had been too long-winded, incoherent and uninteresting. Too long-winded, no doubt: Jean-Paul Burger says that Coillard was given the nickname 'Mungole' by the Lozi population, meaning 'the never-ending rains', an obvious reference to his lengthy sermons. Incoherent and uninteresting, certainly not, for what kept the attention of his audiences were his narratives and anecdotes. What's more, Coillard spoke without the grandiloquence of the times and with a certain modesty, evidence of his humanity. "Initially, no sign indicates the force of his personality", wrote Auguste Sabatier, who entertained Coillard at the theology faculty in Paris on 16 December 1896. "Mr. Coillard is of below average height; one is struck first by his long white beard, flowing to the middle of his chest. But very soon a certain charm operates. Beneath this frail appearance, a profound spirit can be glimpsed in the deep, bright expression of his eyes. His lips are thin and tight indicating that nothing will come from them that has not been deeply pondered within. Over his features is a veil of resigned, sad tenderness ; the look of a man, sojourning in this world with its joys, miseries and beauties, as a pilgrim casting his eyes yonder."

At the time of his visit to Paris, Coillard took part in the creation of the 'Prayer Union for Missions' which recalled the former forgotten tradition of prayer for the Paris Mission. Prayer subjects were collected by a member of the Union and were given to the director of the Mission House who eventually published the list in the JDME and the Petit Messager des Missions. This organisation (which Boegner, who counted on Coillard 'to put the churches back in contact with the Mission in its simplicity', had wanted), was without doubt instrumental in enabling the evangelical movement in the churches to mobilise in favour of the Zambezi.

The pietistic sensitivity of this approach gave them a sense of closeness to a mission that seemed less concerned with political and colonial agitation than others. Ultimately, if the Mission to Madagascar overshadowed the Zambezi Mission, it also helped by stimulating a wide support base. The more evangelical Protestants could support the Zambezi spiritually and materially, whereas others, more politically and liberally inclined, could turn to Madagascar.

### The organisation of the 'Zambezias'

Throughout 1897, Coillard was accompanied on his speaking his tours by captain Alfred Bertrand and Louis Jalla. The latter left for the Zambezi in February 1898, but Alfred Bertrand faithfully continued to accompany Coillard.

Alfred Bertrand, a captain of the Swiss Army, had spent several months in the Lozi country (June-September 1895) as part of a British expedition to Central Africa. Having befriended the missionaries, he was present at the opening of the Lelui Conference, where Coillard was so ill. He was thus a witness to the conditions in which they lived and worked. His letters were published in the Journal de Genève: "What a powerful lesson is given by these pioneers of the Gospel, forever hard at work and giving of themselves. How important it is for Europe to take an interest in and support these missionaries, for theirs is a civilising mission, in the full sense of the word."

Bertrand reiterated this opinion when he met with the Board on 4 May 1896, a few days before Coillard's return to France. He was then able to measure the difficulties in which the Paris Mission found itself and, when he learnt of the sum needed by Coillard and the number of people requested, he decided to support him actively by accompanying him on his speaking engagements.

This tandem is interesting for many reasons. When speaking, they shared out the roles: Bertrand was the impartial explorer, Coillard the missionary. This gave the Zambezi adventures a relatively objective basis on which Coillard could build his own message. The two men very soon realised that they could not count on the Paris Mission Board to attain their objectives.

Bertrand's outlook was that of a certain number of wealthy, well-travelled people: that is, the Boards of the Mission Societies should not be bothered with financial questions. It was for laymen to find the funds and to organise themselves and see to it that they were regularly collected. Coillard's position, according to the tradition of the Paris Mission, was rather to seek funds through the network of auxiliary committees and churches, so that all church members would feel concerned.

But, from the start, Coillard had to face the hard fact that: "We have auxiliary committees; but in many cases, if they work, they do not work well. These committees should be more than simple organisations; they should be a focus of mission life. If Paris is the central 'telegraphic office' of mission, what prevents the installation of small, local lines of communication with our far-away stations and their workers? We missionaries appreciate the personal links just as much as you, our friends, and I don't think this is wrong."

Without actually mentioning it, Coillard was in fact describing the network of 'Zambezias' being set up by Alfred Bertrand wherever they went. By January 1 1898, there were already 18 of these Zambezias: six in France, five in Alsace, seven in Switzerland, linked to each other through a secretariat in Geneva, run by Edouard Favre, and by a new periodical Les nouvelles du Zambèze (News of the Zambezi). According to Alfred Bertrand, the network "consisted of groups which are flexible and organised according to the area where they happen to be… but share the same practical aim: to reach annually the target each Zambezia has set itself… and it is these sums, sent to the Board of the Paris Mission, earmarked for the Zambezi, which form the basis of a secure budget enabling the missionaries to forge ahead."

The Board waited a year before expressing itself officially on the Zambezias. An article in the JDME in May 1898 referred to them as though everyone knew of their existence. It was noted that in the case of the Zambezi, as for other fields, "there is no basic objection to the fact that friends particularly interested in this work should create, not a board of directors – the management is one and indivisible (sic) – but their own fund-raising associations in favour of a particular aspect of the work that they wish to support."

The Board thus agreed on the principle of the 'Zambezias', but was wary of the risk that the unity of the PMS might be threatened by these undertakings. On 7 February 1898, with Coillard and Bertrand present, the question of whether a member of the Board could take part in the creation of a Zambezia in Paris was raised. The answer was that he could not take part as a member of the Board; nevertheless it was felt better that Zambezias be created in agreement with the Board rather than without it, and the creation of a Zambezia in Paris might serve 'to neutralise the over-centralising tendency of the Geneva Zambezia' (sic). It is noteworthy that at this same Board meeting, the question arose of creating auxiliary associations for Madagascar and that, on this subject, the Board feared a take-over by the liberals.

Coillard wrote to Boegner shortly after the 7 February meeting. While delighted with the success of Bertrand's campaign he was not openly supportive of the Zambezias, which their promoter perceived as a lack of enthusiasm: "My field of work is on another level and I would not wish to depreciate in the Churches the mission God has confided in me ... What I appreciate in the Zambezias is the spiritual co-operation of so many friends. There lies the true strength." In fact, the Zambezias were a great success. Thanks to them, Coillard's expedition was financed and, from there on, the treasury of the Zambezi was assured. In August 1898, there were around sixty Zambezias in fourteen European countries and a hundred by 1904.

## Publication of 'Sur le Haut Zambèze' ('On the Threshold of Central Africa')

For a long time, the Board had encouraged Coillard to publish a book on the Zambezi. In 1888, Théophile Jousse offered to write the book himself. He, who had previously vigorously opposed the founding of the Zambezi Mission, was by then convinced of its merits. Though the Board did not finance its publication, the book appeared end-1889, a few days before his death. It is noteworthy that apart from a book by Edouard Jacottet in 1896 on the languages of the Upper Zambezi, no other book had been published on that Mission.

As soon as he arrived in France, Coillard started work on an edition of his letters, which had already appeared in the JDME. His niece, Catherine W. Mackintosh, translated them for the English edition, and Raoul Allier helped in the work of revision and correction of the proofs. The book appeared in London in 1897 entitled 'On the Threshold of Central Africa' and, at the beginning of 1898, with the title 'Sur le Haut Zambèze', a de-luxe edition on glossy paper and with forty printed plates was published in Paris.

It was an immediate best-seller in both countries. The Board then decided to publish a cheaper edition at a more accessible price and to present it to the Académie Française hoping to win one of its annual prizes. The book was recommended for the Montyon prize but did not win it.

The immediate result of this publication, as noted by the Protestant press in general, was that at last people could now get an overall picture of the missionary work in Zambezi over the last twelve years, previously only available to the few readers of the JDME. All the papers underlined the epic nature of this work and counted it among the great epics of humanity, similar to "the Iliad and the Odyssey" (D. Lortsch in the *Evangelist*), the Acts of the Apostles (A. Sabatier in *Journal de Genève*), the Huguenot Resistance (H. Jacottet in *Le Signal*), the explorations of Livingstone and Serpa Pinto ( X in *La Revue des Deux Mondes*).

The Protestant church press (*L'Evangeliste*, *Le Christianisme au XIXe siècle*, *L'Eglise Libre*) underlined the progress that the Gospel had brought to the Lozi people, systematically recalling their barbaric habits, beliefs and institutions; the lay Protestant press (Le Signal) and the secular press (*Le Temps*) underlined the risks for this people of colonial conquest and portrayed the missionaries as their defenders. "The problem is huge" wrote the chronicler in 'Menus Propos' in LeTemps on 28 February 1898, evoking the perils of colonisation, "not only for the Christian conscience but for human reason". "Africa has been partitioned and will be handed over mercilessly to the powers that be. But the question is whether this take-over and this development will occur in conditions that will not be shameful for the 20th century. For this, we are all jointly responsible. Has this been considered?"

The British press was full of praise for Coillard's book, saying it was one of the best travel narratives in the United Kingdom, and that its author should take his place alongside national heroes such as Moffat and Livingstone which, for a Frenchman, was quite an honour.

Through the publication of this book in two languages on the eve of his return to Africa, Coillard testified to a work begun which, with the support of the churches and the sympathy of wider circles, he would carry forward in the eyes of the world, and in the name of France. Was this not precisely the legitimacy that Coillard had come in search of in Europe?

## The baptism of Stephen (Etienne) Semondji

It will be remembered that Mwanangombe, the first Lozi baptised by Coillard, had left to serve Lewanika in 1898. Since then, no other Lozi had been baptised. But on 20 February 1898, Stephen Semondji, one of the boys accompanying Coillard, was baptised at the 'Maison des Missions' in Paris. The accounts of Semondji's profession of faith and his reception at the Mission House were published in the JDME in March 1898, signifying the symbolic nature of this sacramental act for the Zambezi Mission.

Semondji's profession of faith appears in a letter sent to Coillard, where he calls him 'my father'. It is an Africanised version of the parable of the prodigal son. In the parable, the focus is on the father (natural father and spiritual father as the image of God). In Semondji's interpretation and in Coillard's commentaries, the image of Simondji's natural parents (father and mother) gives way to that of his spiritual parents (Coillard and his wife), with the blessing of Lewanika as the eldest son.

Semondji recounts how, entering Coillard's service against his wish, he was forever running away from them and from school and returning to his parents. With his father's consent, he set out on a hunting trip, but very soon, he felt hungry and was ambushed. Miraculously freed, he returned home and his mother fulfilled his wish to return to the Coillards. There, Christina Coillard told him the story of the prodigal son and Semondji knew that he should convert. Shortly after, Christina Coillard and his parents passed away. This orphan son thus became Coillard's most faithful servant and offered to accompany him on his journey to hospital in Kimberley. Before leaving the country, Lewanika told Semondji : "Your father is dead, and your mother too, you are an orphan", and pointing to Coillard, he added: "Here is your father, but remember, he is not only yours, he is the father of the nation, my very own; bind yourself to him and take care of him for us all."

One can imagine how this story impressed the people present at Semondji's baptism. Semondji, the second Lozi to be baptised, received the significantly meaningful name of Etienne (Stephen). The editor of the JDME, none other than Alfred Boegner, interpreted this touching and solemn ceremony in the following way: "Let us express our gratitude and simply observe here that with this baptism, a new pact is sealed between us and this young brother, his nation and the mission that brought him to Jesus Christ. This baptism, celebrated at the heart of our Society, creates for us a specific obligation: we must adopt Semondji and surround him with our prayers and our affection."

The idea of a biblical covenant, contracted between a people and the mission which grew in Lesotho, is evoked here. It is not surprising that Coillard and Boegner applied it to the Zambezi. Considering the situation of the mission, the two men felt the need to renew that covenant as it had, to a certain extent, been betrayed three times:

- Mwanangombe's departure together with many other Mission workers.
- By Lewanika's behaviour, which was far from on a par with that of Moshoshoe.
- By the irresponsibility of the French churches which had not sent a single missionary in 12 years.

After Semondji's baptism and the appointment of Jacques Liénard, the ordained French minister, Coillard could once more feel truly called by Lewanika and supported by the Paris Mission. In these conditions, the Zambezi Mission appeared to be definitely established, and the covenant between the Mission, the Lozi nation and the churches of France definitively sealed.

# V

## THE EXPEDITIONS OF 1898 AND 1899

The focus above on Coillard's stay in Europe does not imply that nothing was happening on the shores of the Zambezi. But, for two years Coillard's speaking tours in Europe had dominated the media and somewhat overshadowed any information coming from the Lozi country.

A significant example is that a few weeks before Semondji's baptism, on 6 January 1898, four adult baptisms took place at Lealui, three of which were requested by pupils of the Bible School. They were thus the first to be baptised since Mwanangombe's baptism in 1890. There is no doubt that Coillard knew nothing of this on the day Semondji was baptised. Judging from the extant correspondence, it was only towards the end of the first term of 1898 that the Board heard of it. In a report to the General Assembly on 18 April 1898, a vague mention of 'pagans having been baptised' is made, immediately followed by the statement: "No doubt, the return of the founder of the Mission will be the signal for an energetic renewal of every aspect of their work."

During the two years when Coillard was on his speaking tours, the news from Europe upheld the mission in Africa. It looked forward to reinforcements while struggling on with the usual problems: lack of food supplies, threats of war and cattle disease. Such was the case for Paolo Davit who, despite ill-health, volunteered in early 1897 to organise a search for supplies as far away as Palapye, the railway terminus from the Cape, where he hoped to meet up with the Coïssons, the Merciers and Levi, a Sotho evangelist. They did meet in April but Davit was exhausted. Following unpleasant disagreements over transport and with Mwanangombe, he took refuge in Lesotho before returning to Italy.

### A. The 'small-scale' Coïsson and Jalla expeditions of 1898
Once Davit had left, the Coïssons, Merciers and Levi decided to move on to the Zambezi, but the expedition came to grief as the oxen died of plague. Forced to abandon their baggage train in the desert, they returned to Palapye in August 1897. The Merciers fell ill and went to Lesotho before returning to Switzerland. On the edge of the desert, the Coïssons and the Levis awaited the dry season and the arrival of Louis Jalla's expedition, which had left Europe in March 1898. In fact, this expedition was able to reach Bulawayo by the newly-extended railway line. The Coïssons, unable to leave their baggage in the desert any longer, decided

to set off on their own in ox-drawn wagons. The two groups met up at Deka and, on 28 June 1898, together reached Kazungula where, from 21 July to 8 August, the 6th Mission conference was held.

Thus, for the first time, fifteen missionaries were together in the Lozi country. In spite of two new upsets (the deaths of 5 month-old Jeanne, the Boiteux's first child and Eliza Kanedi Paulus, the Lealui evangelist's wife), they confirmed their trust in the future: "Our small numbers and the distance between us was till now a weapon in the hands of Satan. Today, our small army is growing, the chain of our stations is made of tighter links and we can return to the fray with more courage and more ardour. May God make it more successful."

Two new stations were to be founded: the first near the Victoria Falls, with the imminent establishment at Livingstone of the railway terminus from the Cape. Kazungula, having lost its importance, was to become an annex of the new station. The other station was Senanga, the new link between Sesheke and Sefula-Lealui. The Senanga station would be occupied by the Boiteux family only in November 1898 and the station at the Falls by the Coïsson family a year later. On both stations, despite agreements with the local chiefs and the British Resident, the missionaries were obliged to build their houses and the station themselves.

While awaiting the arrival of Coillard's grand expedition, the Mission once more experienced bereavement and desertion: the death on 1 September 1898 of Ernestina, the wife of Willie Mokalapa, the Sotho evangelist from Lealui, and on 27 March 1899, that of Marie Jalla, Louis' wife (this family had already lost three children and two others had been left in Italy during their leave). The Sotho evangelists, Kaneli and Mokalapa returned to Lesotho following the deaths of their wives; Eugénie Specht, the schoolteacher at Lealui, left after marrying, on 16 May 1899, a missionary of the Primitive Methodists Mission.

However, there were a few signs of positive developments on the horizon: the death on 29 September 1898, of Mwauluka, Lewanika's Ngambela (prime minister) since 1885. "He represented the conservative party, opposed to the Mission, the Protectorate and the granting of concessions – sometimes known as the pagan party by the Mission – and whose influence prevented the king from becoming a Christian," wrote J.P. Burger. Mukamba was appointed in his place. He was 31, close to Lewanika and to Prince Litia, one of the first converts. Litia was baptised on Coillard's return on 26 June 1899. These men made up what was known as the Christian Party, on which Lewanika counted to promote his social reform: the struggle against private revenge and accusation of witchcraft by the establishment of a police corps; the struggle against alcohol, by forbidding the brewing of traditional beer; the emancipation of the women who had become Christian (one of whom, Nolianga, belonged to the group baptised on 6 January 1898).

On 16 February 1899, Mukamba was installed in his functions as Ngambela and on 30 March was baptised with seven other candidates. On the same day, the first two Lozi evangelists Filipi Nyundo and Samuele Silvendo, both pupils of the Lealui school, were granted church office, replacing the Sotho evangelists who had returned to their country.

On the eve of the arrival of Coillard's expedition, these long-awaited conversions provoked a wave of optimism in Paris: "If God could at last fulfil the prayers and efforts of Mr. Coillard that Lewanika be converted (JDME, June 1899), the evangelisation of the Zambezi could, with the arrival of the strong team we have had the joy of sending, forge ahead with great strides."

### B. The group of seventeen: a disaster

Having left England on 10 December 1898 together with Samata, Semondji and Alfred Bertrand, Coillard first visited Lesotho before reaching Bulawayo, where seventeen missionaries were to join him on the way to the Zambezi through the desert. On arrival at Mafeking on 9 March 1899, he received a telegram from Alfred Boegner telling of his planned arrival and his intention of accompanying them to Bulawayo.

This moved Coillard to write in his journal: "Mr Boegner will see for himself, and the Board in Paris together with our friends will see through him, the use that is made of the funds entrusted to me, and everyone will understand how much more pleasant and easy it is to collect money penny by penny, franc by franc, instead of spending by shillings and pounds".

On 20 March 1899, everyone met in the Imperial Hotel for a last evening together, during which the twenty people present signed a card headed: 'Tout pour le Roi' ('Our all for the King').

The expedition was composed of the following Europeans: five pastors, four of whom were married: Jacques and Madeleine Liénard from France, Juste and Marie Bouchet, Roderich and Eva de Prosch from Geneva, Paul and Alice Ramseyer, Théophile Burnier from Vaud, Switzerland; a French administrator and his wife, Elie and Hélène Lemue; a French schoolteacher, Eva Dupuy; three artisans, of whom two were married: Henri and Louise Martin and Théophile Verdier from France, Emile and Elise Rittener from Switzerland.

Most of them came from the Free Churches in both countries, and had responded to Coillard's calls during his speaking tours. Roderich de Prosch was a doctor as well. He had been lent to the Paris Mission by the Swiss Society for Assistance to African Slaves. This society was dissolved after the enquiry led by Samuel Junod in Senegal. The Society was then handed over to the Zambezi Mission. All these people were young, between nineteen and thirty-three. Most of the couples were married on the eve of their departure.

One should note that for the first time since the founding of the Mission, the French were in the majority. At the farewell meeting on 5 February 1899, in the Oratoire du Louvre in Paris, Jean Bianquis had emphasised the fact that four of these young French women carried in their veins blood from the Cévennes or from Poitou, traditionally Protestant French provinces, thus bringing to the Zambezi Mission a new spirit, that of the Huguenot woman. He declared: "I congratulate these young sisters who have come to work for the conversion of the heathen in a country under the British Protectorate. They will somehow repay an old debt – that owed by the Churches of France to so many excellent and loving Christian women, be they English or Scottish, who since the beginning of the century have worked towards the evangelisation of our people. As we know, to work for the spread of the Word is always an honour and a proof of expansion. Let us widen our hearts and our actions, thereby proving that the sap of the old Protestant tree is not spent."

On 22 March 1899, a column of twenty-one wagons, drawn by 330 oxen driven by sixty Africans, started out for a journey of two months through semi-desert regions. "This journey was rich in adventures" wrote Edouard Favre, "of the kind common to all journeys in Africa. Of no surprise to Coillard, they were new to the joyful young travellers: wagons bogged down or overturned, broken shafts, dangerous fords, lack of water, roads lost or hard to find, deep forests, bottomless sands, more or less successful hunting and even imaginary lions." But death rapidly prowled round the caravans. The day they left, one of the African drivers died and, on arrival on the banks of the Zambezi on Whitsunday, they heard the news that Marie Jalla had passed away. From Sesheke on 16 June, Coillard wrote: "So we have a new grave, a new Macpela added to so many others. For us, it's another confirmation of our taking possession of a country which has received and conserved the ashes of our beloved ones."

The newcomers' evangelical commitment no doubt enabled them to accept uncritically such an interpretation of the death of a woman of only

35, who had already seen three of her children die while she was among the first reinforcements of the Mission. But, when on 18 June, Marie Bouchet succumbed to a malaria-attack at nineteen, after less than a month in Lozi country, despondency overcame her travelling companions. Juste Bouchet, her husband, aged 22, expressed their thinking in a letter to Boegner, recalling the joyous evening on 20 March in Bulawayo: "For us, at that time, there was no merit in being joyful while on the road to the land of privations. We knew that many had left never to return; but we were not them. We recognised we might die in the Zambezi; but we and our loved ones, did we really believe that we would be hit? We were happy, less because we were 'dedicated', but because we were all young, truly young. We had our illusions. Who can blame us? But the Master was obliged to rid us of our illusions... All the same, in the anguish of which I have spoken, never for a moment did the idea come to me that I had perhaps been mistaken in leaving and taking her with me... My conscience is free on that subject; even if my wife was still so young, it was nevertheless in faithfulness to God's calling that she came with me. It was her own conviction; it is mine more than ever despite the blow that has stricken and taken her from me."

This letter is admirable for the courage and lucidity of his faith, but even more for the lack of recrimination against the Paris Mission and the *Zambezias*. In the circumstances, they carry a heavy responsibility in having let this young crowd forge ahead in the face of terrible perils.

It was only after three more deaths (Emile Rittener, artisan of Sefula on 10 December 1899, Leonie Martin, the wife of the other craftsman in Sesheke, on 17 February 1900, Eva Dupuy, the Sesheke teacher on 15 April) and repatriation for health reasons of six others (Elise Rittener and her baby, Paul and Alice Ramseyer, Elie and Hélène Lemue) that, for the first time, in July 1900, the Board decided together with the Geneva Zambezi Commission, with Alfred Bertrand present, to reinforce in future the necessary health measures to lessen the risks of illness and death. These included improved in-depth medical examinations for the candidates, a review of whether to send out young people, considering the fact that most married on the eve of departure and their first child was often born shortly after arrival, improvement of hygiene and increased food supplies, the building of better housing, etc.

While certain measures, particularly those concerning the missionaries in the field, had to be implemented rapidly, the Board decided to deal with this serious subject only in September. For the time being, they were concerned with the fate and status of the repatriates who had left the

Mission field for health reasons, before their official leave and without permission from the Board. Among other difficulties this involved a financial question.

During the several meetings in autumn 1900, the Board replied to a letter from the Lealui Conference (February 1900) asking for reinforcements to replace the deceased, the repatriated, and Emma and Adolphe Jalla, on leave. The health problem was on the agenda again when the Board considered the possibility of setting up a health centre for missionaries in Bulawayo. The application by Dr Georges Reutter from Switzerland was considered. He insisted that the living conditions be healthy and that stints not last more than six years.

The Board carried on its work, but the serious health problems were not addressed. It focused instead on rumours of the return of Georges Mercier, the last artisan in the Lozi country, in order to acquire in Europe a steam engine for the Sefula trade school, and spent long hours discussing this. Then came the news of his death 18 October 1900; this put en end to their criticism of this missionary, although the letter reproaching the Conference for letting him leave without proper authorisation had already been sent.

The announcement in May 1901 of the death of Jacques Liénard on 7 March finally induced the Board to, at last, take measures on matters of health. Although unaware at the time of Maggie Mann's death 14 May 1901 in the desert between Kazungula and Bulawayo, the executive committee prepared a declaration concerning 'the attitude to be taken in the JDME with regard to the questions raised here and there among the public concerning the future of the Zambezi. It thought it wiser not to enter into any discussion on the subject.'

## C. Arousal of public opinion, press interference and the Board's health policy

It is easy to imagine that with regular news of deaths and repatriations, the churches and mission friends felt most concerned. Although the JMDE sent messages of sympathy and sorrow, it was to be expected that, faced with the deaths and the repatriations of so many young people, doubts arose and protests were soon heard about the validity of such expeditions.

A letter signed 'S.M., a friend of Missions and missionaries' which appeared in *Christianisme au 19e siècle* on 7 September 1899, for the first time brought the debate concerning death in the Mission field into the open. 'S.M.', who was perfectly well informed about the affairs of the

Paris Mission, started his article by giving the names and ages of the seven missionaries who had died in one year, most of them young women, five in the Zambezi, one in Senegal and one in the Congo. Then he drew the lesson from this hecatomb: "This will certainly raise strong protests from Christians who, casting aside the laws of physics... and of human liberty...throw the responsibility on God and see his hand everywhere, as though he were the sole artisan of our fate. I am sorry, but I cannot accept that theology. Far am I from concluding as does the editor of the JDME (June 1900) that: 'It is through their tombs that the Kingdom of God takes possession of new territories...' Rather I would say with Jesus in the desert: 'You shall not tempt the Lord your God.' Because, in my opinion, sending to deadly countries young men and women, not yet 30 or 35 years of age, totally unaccustomed to tropical climates, means imposing a miracle on God, thus tempting Him. Yet God, who tempts nobody, will not allow himself to be tempted by anyone. Thus they are sent to a pointless, premature death, that God, who is not Moloch, cannot impose on his children."

The debate did not end there; the following week another person, L.C. (why the anonymity? Were people fearful of holding such opinions?) fully concurred with S.M. and went still further, scathingly referring to these honeymoons in jolting wagons and primitive trains imposed on the young missionaries. However, the interesting thing about this letter was that its criticisms were based on a reading between the lines of the book by Jacques Liénard 'Our Journey' which seems to have foreseen that the expedition would be a disaster.

Liénard felt compelled to answer. On 25 November 1900, he sent a letter to Christianisme which appeared on 1 March 1901. The missionary does not contest the interpretation of his book: "I am grateful to L.C. for pinpointing the issue of sending out young couples immediately after their marriage. He has said what none of us had the right to say and he has understood what I could only imply about the disastrous conditions of this situation. In any case, the terrible and painful lessons drawn from our bereavement have been understood by all, missionaries and directors... What is important now is not to continue to lament on 'our tribulations', to tell our friends that mission comes at a price, that it costs what it must; or to try to bring together the partisans of two implacable theodicies."

Liénard concludes by commenting on missionary methods in the Zambezi, referring to the system inherited from Lesotho of a chain of stations, combined with that of the English in Uganda, with a limited number of centres which are extended through pastors, evangelists and black teachers. He recognised that the Lozi country had no such networks of stations or established centres. Thus, taking into consideration the loss of lives endured, the Mission was confronted with enormous challenges: how to prevent an exodus of young Lozis, engaged to work in the mining companies and at risk of falling under the influence of the Ethiopians (see following pages) and of leaving the Mission? Liénard's suggested solutions included combining the upper primary school with its English class, started a year earlier by Alfred Mann in Lealui, with the trade school at Sefula. Since Waddell's departure, it had been in a state of abandon, but Georges Mercier had put it back on its feet. But, by the time Liénard had planned this, these establishments were no longer operative.

The Board never mentioned a word about this correspondence. Why? It could not, without contradicting itself, admit that the young missionary was right. Its answer came indirectly through the publication of a letter from Coillard in the JDME in December 1899. For months, no word had been heard from Coillard. Now, breaking his silence, he wondered if the expedition had not been a mistake: "It could be, in the light of the sombre events of the last 12 months, that the 17-member expedition appears to some of our friends to have been a reckless enterprise and even a profound mistake". But, as usual, Coillard answered his own question. The more he pondered over it, the more convinced was he that God had inspired this courageous enterprise and had led him and his companions. And repeating his favourite comparison between war and the mission, he adds: "We organise the ambulances long before singing the Te Deum of victory. Our recruits had to go through the baptism of fire. It was necessary for their sakes and it is necessary for those that will follow." It seems quite clear that the Board identified with such a position. Apparently not a single voice was raised against it.

Jacques Liénard's death revived the polemics raised by the press earlier in which, as mentioned above, the Board had decided not to engage. This time, several papers raised the alarm:

-    *The Witness* (Le Témoignage), Lutheran: "O Lord! How much longer? Such is the cry that bursts from our heart, when we have to announce yet another death, and not the least, yet one more in the Zambezi!... We cannot understand; and more than ever, we realise that the ways of God are not our ways."

-    *L'Eglise libre*: "Recklessness and light-heartedness cannot mean faith," wrote Edouard Soulier, "and walking by faith means first taking account of previous experience, of lessons learnt, of previous discoveries and adding – what the Christian alone is capable of – the perception of the invisible." Soulier reckoned that in continuing to send reinforcements to the Zambezi such as Albert and Julie Lageard (April 1901), a young Italian couple under 30, the Board was once more guilty of imprudence. After making a number of suggestions concerning health measures, he concluded: "Even though we know that God can make good out of our errors, our hearts are weary of useless and premature losses. No one can decimate and discourage a generation just entering into the Master's service."

The Board could no longer remain totally silent in the face of such declarations. But it did not wish to enter into a debate on theodicy, as suggested by Liénard, nor did it wish to be told what to do. It made an attempt to discern the lessons learnt from the events, and to establish rules and indications for the future in an article in the JDME of July 1901 entitled 'Concerning our bereavement'. First of all, the Board wished to thank all those who had sent messages of sympathy to the directors of the Paris Mission, thus underlining that the grief was theirs as well. As for the messages coming from the families concerned, the Board insisted that not a single protest or recrimination was made. They were "an example of surrender, of fraternal sympathy, and consolation for ourselves."

The Board then made it clear that it understood that the churches, while not putting their support in the balance, wanted to be "reassured that the best and wisest use would be made of the resources and lives of those that were sent out on the work of its mission." Also, the Board sought to show that it had not waited for the current problems to occur to occupy itself with the concerns currently raised by public opinion. Several doctors, including Jules de Seynes (president of the Paris Mission) were involved in drawing up health measures. Some of these were already applied in Senegal and the Congo: stronger and fewer stations, more frequent leaves, more staff and healthier housing. Nevertheless, the Board was obliged to explain the delay concerning the Lozi country. It invoked three reasons:

- The influence of the Lesotho example on which the missionaries had based their work.
- The distances and difficulties of travel which rendered that example almost totally inapplicable.
- The resources of the churches were limited by the pioneers of the Mission.

Finally the Board tried to make the authors of the numerous criticisms and suggestions, including in the press, understand that not all were well-founded. Such was the case, for example, of a period of acclimatisation in a non-tropical area, and of not accepting missionaries under the age of thirty. The Board added that it was not infallible, that accidents could occur due to exhaustion or carelessness. In the end, the best precaution was action, by increasing the numbers of missionaries, and requiring them to follow the new set of rules soon to be in place.

It was clear that the Board would not give up an iota of its authority with regard to mission work and its ultimate destiny. Nevertheless, it defined the limits of its responsibility vis-à-vis the deaths which had occurred, and endeavoured to take the initiative as far as mission strategy was concerned, something it had been unable to do as long as the Zambezi mission, until the disastrous expedition of the seventeen, was directed and led by a single person.

Yet once again a death, this time of Eva de Prosch on 13 September 1901, forced the Board to come out into the open. At the meeting of the Zambezi Commission on 18 November 1901, Pastor Roger Hollard insisted that Boegner publish the new instructions. The public and the churches needed to know. "Our whole work depends on it", he said. Thus, the following month, the Board published in the JDME a letter to the Zambezi conference listing the measures decided upon that summer. The letter is preceded by a special notice: "We are not in the habit of publishing correspondence between ourselves and our Mission. It appears necessary to make an exception… it will show our friends the extent to which the Board has shared, and in some ways foreseen, the concerns of our Churches with regard to our Missions in tropical countries". This letter marked in certain ways a radical reversal in the strategy of the P.M.S. with regard to the Lozi country:

- It suggested measures to concentrate on the more important outposts, and to entrust the minor posts to local fellow-workers.
- It requested the preparation of a plan of action concentrating on strengthening a few stations with more Europeans, instead of maintaining a number with a single European. The letter underlined that this new plan implied a break with the former Lesotho-style strategies so far applied in the Zambezi.
- New health regulations were to be followed regarding the age and marriage of missionaries, healthier housing, acclimatisation and convalescent homes, etc. The letter also announced the arrival of a Swiss doctor, Georges Reutter, who was coming to study how to improve the living and working conditions of the missionaries.

With these measures, taken after the tragic events and deep concern of Mission friends, the Zambezi Mission based on the Lesotho model seemed to die a second death. The first time had been in 1880 when the Lesotho Church had refused to support the Zambezi enterprise. The Zambezi Mission had become autonomous, and what autonomy! But François Coillard, its new father, a son of Lesotho, had followed the same pattern and taken with him a number of workers who had also paid their tribute to malaria. In 1901, it was decided once again to give up the Lesotho methods; this did not mean that the two missions would not co-operate, but on a different basis. This raised another question: what would become of the Sotho workers in the Lozi country, and of Coillard himself, in the new Zambezi Mission at the dawn of the 20th century?

### D. The Ethiopians and Coillard's death

On returning from his long leave in Europe, Coillard found that the Sotho evangelists Willie Mokalapa and Paulus Kanedi, both widowers, had recently left on leave to Lesotho. Reaching Lealui on 18 September 1899, he read two letters from Willie Mokalapa; one, to Adolphe Jalla, was full of gratitude for the support received on the death of his wife and for the letters of recommendation provided by the missionary. The second letter was for Lewanika who had inadvertently asked Jalla to translate it. It contained complaints against the Mission and boosted the principles of Ethiopianism. Mokalapa promised to return to the Lozi country with money and tools to build new schools including a technical college. The king welcomed the news, since over the last two years the work of the Mission had slowed down, and the station at Sefula, where a technical college was to be built, was in ruins.

The Ethiopans had previously tried to influence the Lesotho Church without success. Their passage in the country was short-lived and their influence practically nil, since in October 1899, the Conference and the Synod had decided together to stand up to them. Willie Mokalapa was present and even made a vehement speech against them.

According to Maurice Leenhardt, a Mission ethnologist who had heard of this from Adolphe Jalla, Mokalapa had had contact with the Ethiopians before leaving the Lozi country and his mixed messages were meant to mislead the missionaries. In this way, he could ensure his return to Lesotho in case the help he had promised Lewanika fell through. This meant that with Mokalapa's assistance the 'Ethiopians' had serious plans for the Lozi country. This prospect worried Coillard: "The shadow of the Ethiopian church is stretching over us and in the most unexpected way," he wrote to Mission friends in April 1900. "We had no idea that Willie and Paul were aware of the movement which was troubling the churches of South Africa." Maurice Leenhardt studied the way Ethiopianism had influenced a man like Willie and suggested three reasons for it:

- The inadequate salaries of the evangelists,
- The lack of real sharing by the missionaries, especially in times of famine,
- The lack of respect from local people for them, compared to the consideration given to evangelists in Lesotho.

According to Leenhardt, only the third reason was tenable. But these recriminations hide more basic claims: to be freed from missionary control and to trust the evangelisation of Africa to the Africans themselves.

From 1880 onwards, several dissident pastors from Wesleyan or Anglican missions in southern Africa, together with other malcontents, had founded independent churches here and there. The best known one was the Ethiopian Church founded by a dissident Wesleyan pastor from Pretoria, Manghena Mokone, who was soon to be joined by James Dwane, another dissident Wesleyan pastor from Port Elizabeth. These new churches had no hope of obtaining legal recognition in the Cape Colony nor in the Boer Republics. Hearing that an important Black Church existed in America, the Ethiopians contacted it and in 1896, Dwane went to the United States and encountered the African Methodist Episcopal Church (AMEC) led by Bishop Henry Turner. For 10 years Turner had tried to extend evangelisation to southern Africa in the context of his project of evangelisation of the African continent by black Americans, as had been done in Liberia in 1833 by the Methodist Episcopal Mission.

On returning to Africa, Dwane tried to have the AMEC recognised and hoped that the churches with Ethiopian leanings would create a new church whose key-note would be 'Africa for Christ'. He invited Bishop Turner to come over and help him organise his church, as he was meeting with difficulties from, on the one hand, the Afrikaners who feared the self-rule of the Ethiopians, and on the other from the missionaries who felt their work was threatened. Turner arrived in South Africa in 1898 and, while he helped organise the Ethiopian Church, he won the sympathy of the missionary world. Co-operation with the AMEC seemed possible, as had occurred elsewhere.

According to Leenhardt, Turner's success was due to his title of Bishop, to his diplomatic ways, to the warmth of his voice and his serious philanthropic spirit. He even promised a great university for Blacks, half of which would be paid for by Americans, and the other half by Africans themselves. A piece of land was even bought at Queenstown.

But after Turner's departure, the Ethiopians fell back on their persistent idea of emancipation from the missionary world. However, having been to a certain extent recognised by the whites, the movement had to invent a peaceful strategy towards the missionaries. Leenhardt identifies two ways:

*Preaching*

"they could not openly accuse the missionaries of being malevolent political agents. One must grant that they did not preach hatred: they based their arguments on some fanciful exegesis of Bible texts and on the fatal weaknesses of European missionaries." Leenhardt quotes, for example, a letter from the Pretoria Conference of April 1899 to the bishops in America: "It would be unwise on the part of Africans to expect more of the missionaries and it would be foolish on their part to imagine that they can do more."

*Secret correspondence*

"the means of extending their influence lay in their secret correspondence, some of which fell into missionary hands." This is the kind of letter that Willie had sent to Lewanika, dazzling him with the idea of a new church, well provided with funds, and with qualified church and technical staff.

What hurt Coillard most about this was Lewanika's double-dealing: "Willie had already let him into his confidence, before leaving the country; he cleared himself of this by saying he thought those plans were fully approved of by us." Indeed, on returning from Europe, Coillard discovered that Lewanika had already planned to install the Ethiopian school at Lealui, on land that had been granted to the Mission. Coillard was sure that Lewanika meant to create competition between the Mission and the Ethiopian Church. Coillard nevertheless announced his decision to continue to preach the gospel, even in a spirit of controversy.

In fact, Coillard was obsessed with the idea that Willie, his son and former evangelist, might come and settle in Lealui itself. He referred to it in nearly all his letters. He wrote to the Board in November 1900: "Please do not underestimate the matter, as if the natives were incapable of successfully undertaking an important task; that would be a great mistake. Willie and Crammer Matra, who has joined him, are capable men. Willie is very popular here, by the fact that he is black and has a pleasant nature.

He is a very capable school master, a good evangelist and a true Christian."

Jean-Paul Burger correctly questions the reasons for Coillard's attitude: "Was it a matter of age, of weariness and ill-health which made him so apprehensive of the Ethiopians? He feared a campaign of disparagement and slander, reminiscent of Middleton's work. He foresaw that Willie's main aim would be to attract the Christians linked to the Mission, to carry off the pupils who had already acquired the habit of school by promising them better levels of instruction than the Mission had given them." There are no doubt other reasons for this attitude:

- The most immediate cause was that, with the reducation of personnel from the ill-fated 1899 expedition, Coillard feared that the new reinforcements would be insufficient to support what he himself called "the first shock of this terrible concurrence of events." The threat of the arrival of the Ethiopians gave him one more reason to plead for a greater number of collaborators.

- A deeper cause was that several times before, Coillard had written that he would joyfully accept the Ethiopians, were they to come as auxiliaries and after having got rid of what he called their racial prejudice, that is, their hatred of the white man. This clearly meant that Coillard would not accept to be on an equal footing with Africans whom he considered, apart from the prestige of their colour, not up to the demands of the task. Was he right, or had he succumbed to the prejudices of the times which deemed the African to be an incapable underling, unable to manage his affairs? Despite his numerous declarations of deep love for Africa and Africans, it seems that he was unable to establish a relationship other than that of a father – and an over-bearing father – with a son – and a submissive son at that.

For a man of Willie's stamp, proud and sensitive, this paternalistic relationship was unbearable. An alternative attitude, based on collaboration and the surrender of some of his missionary power, was no more bearable for a man like Coillard, whose character resembled that of his opponent. Ensuing events would show that the breakdown of relations between the two was irremediable.

It was only in October 1903 that Willie returned to the Lozi country. Théophile Burnier ironically described his arrival at Sesheke: "This morning, on my way to Litia's, I beheld a clergyman dressed in a black frock coat and waistcoat; one could have mistaken him for a clergyman from London, if it were not for his black face. It was Willie, our former evangelist, who is now 'Director of the Zambezi Mission', with a fancy parchment to vouch for it. As usual, I was dressed in khaki riding trousers and gaiters. There was no doubt that between Willie and me, he was the greater clergyman." This word sketch of their appearance implies that between the black clergyman disguised as a church dignitary and the missionary as an army commander, a conflict of authority was likely to be played out before a bewildered population.

On the way to the Lozi country, François Coillard and Willie Mokalapa had already met at a railway station near Bloemfontein. Coillard had tried to have a discussion with Mokalapa, but the latter had avoided the issue by saying he had a train to catch. "I begged him not to bring trouble to Lealui" wrote Coillard to Edouard Favre "and I assured him that if he settled among his people in an unoccupied area, we could work on good terms and pray for each other."

On arrival at Sesheke on 3 October 1903, Coillard reiterated in writing this time his offer to collaborate. The letter is written in Sotho, addressed to 'my brother', a term he used three times in the letter, reminding him that: "you are our child. Do not kick out against those who brought you up, and don't despise them in the eyes of the heathen." As well, Coillard set out the conditions by which the Ethiopian church should be implanted. "Africa is a vast country and even the territory governed by Lewanika is vast, very vast. If you are indeed burning with zeal for God and for souls, it does not seem necessary that you should trample on us. I would not like us to be on bad terms. Should you settle even at some distance from us, we should strengthen each other with reciprocal respect and affection rather than suffering mutually by spite, thereby destroying the work of God."

On 10 November, Mokalapa replied in English in an official letter using a very dry and at times quite violent tone which seemed disproportionate in comparison with Coillard's remarks, but which showed the extent to which their relationship had deteriorated.

Mokalapa begins by spelling out all his titles, of which there were many: Arch-elder, Overseer, Director of the Training Institute, President of the District Conference, President Elder of Barotseland and Central Africa (sic). His letter is addressed 'To the Rev. F. Coillard, Dear Sir.' He twice states that he has been 'insulted' by the letter he has received and declares: "There is no justification for your opposition to our setting ourselves up in this country as missionaries of the Gospel. There is still room for each Christian denomination in this valley, and especially in this city (Lealui), where dwell hundreds and hundreds of unconverted people. We do not intend to take over your Church members, nor do we want them. In your letter you compare me to a wild animal, a franc tireur, an enemy, etc. Sir, I must tell you that I am a minister of Christ's word, duly ordained according to Holy ordinances. If I respect you as my father, I do not see why you should not respect me as a son. Kindly refrain from this insolence, otherwise I shall have to return the compliment. I have not forgotten your bad treatment of me. Nevertheless I honour you as a father, and you must honour me as a son. There is no controversy. Let us work in harmony. We recognise every Christian denomination on the surface of the earth." The letter ends with a post-scriptum, a veritable death-blow, supported by a Bible verse (Luke 9: 49-50) saying that "God had not sent him (Coillard) here to take over the country and forbid other Christian nations to settle there and in its capital", and that if he wanted to avoid trouble, he must cease slandering his (Mokalapa's) church which is, according to him, perfectly loyal.

The epilogue to this deplorable affair, the terms of which were revealed to French Protestantism in L'Eglise libre (24 June 1904) only after Coillard's death were two-fold.

-       Coillard and Jalla enjoined Lewanika to choose between the Mission and the Ethiopian church at Lealui. Lewanika decided that the Ethiopians should not settle in the capital, but at some distance north of it, which they accepted, no doubt somewhat unwillingly.

-       In November 1903, trouble broke out at the Lealui school and in April 1904, the evangelists went on strike. Some pupils and evangelists complained that they were unable to learn English and wanted to register with the Ethiopians where English was taught. The pupils were forbidden by Litia himself from changing schools, and four evangelists were disciplined by Adolphe Jalla. Once again, thanks to his personal authority, Coillard was able to calm the evangelists and to avoid a schism. On 23 April 1904 he met with them and declared: "You have several masters, but after all you have one only Father. I speak to you as my children, to whom I have given life and love. Do follow my advice."

This is the last battle fought by the father of the Zambezi Mission. A month later he caught black-water fever, the illness which had killed off so many Africans and Europeans in that Mission. On 27 May he passed away in his seventieth year.

On 17 July 1904, during a memorial service at l'Oratoire du Louvre, Alfred Boegner attempted to spell out the heritage the missionary had bequeathed to the PMS and to all Protestantism. This heritage was made up of three parts:

-    *The Zambezi Mission itself*, because it was his own creation; on three occasions Coillard had already bequeathed it to the Paris Mission: by perceiving it as an extension of the Lesotho Mission; by offering it to the Paris Mission from its inception in 1880; and by repeating this offer during his second return to France in 1896.

Boegner then described in a few words the characteristic traits of this Mission. He noted first that, confronted with this inheritance, many friends might be tempted to accept it only after an inventory. Indeed, this Mission presented dangers and difficulties, and the results in comparison with the lives it had cost were minimal. (The first statistics were only revealed in 1906.) It was not an exaggeration to say, at the time of Coillard's death, that in the Zambezi there were probably no more people baptised than there were missionary and evangelist deaths, that is to say some thirty people. But Boegner indignantly contradicted those who seemed to ignore that the Lozi country was the throne of Satan, where reigned absolute power and corruption. In this context, although the results of evangelisation might not have been spectacular, they were nevertheless evident.

-    *An enlarged mission family*: At this point, Boegner underlined that it was thanks to the second generation of Lesotho missionaries, to which Coillard belonged, with reinforcements from French-speaking Switzerland and the Italian Waldensians, and the financial support from a network of friends in Europe, that the Paris Mission had widened its horizons. He added that, thanks to the Zambezi Mission, the Paris Mission had reinforced its internationalism, one of its strong points from the outset with the result that "that great and fruitful solidarity... had impregnated our souls with the spirit of the universal Church".

-    *The missionary spirit*: This was for Boegner the most valuable aspect of the Coillard inheritance. According to Boegner, the missionary spirit was made up of prayer and faith, the one feeding and strengthening the inner life, the other providing the impetus to go forward, regardless of men, their attitudes, their comments, their opinions, but with trust in God, his commands and his promises. According to Boegner, Coillard was an exceptional representative of that spirit.

Of all the speeches made that day, Boegner's was without doubt the most concrete and down-to-earth, allowing a reading of Coillard's life with all its lights and shadows. As for the other speeches and the great number of articles in the British, South African and French press, without exception they praised the memory of Coillard. "A great and noble figure" (*Christianisme au 19e siècle*), "a first-rate Christian" (*Le Signal*), "the Apostle of the Zambezi" (La Vie Nouvelle), "a courageous John the Baptist" (*Le Témoignage*), "an Elijah" (*L'Evangéliste*), "the French Livingstone" (*Le Figaro*), "a great Frenchman" (*Le Relèvement*, Marseille), "the greatest missionary of the Paris Mission Society" (*Revue Internationale des Missions*). In fact, these articles tell us nothing new about the work and personality of Coillard, except for the fact that he had become part of the missionary legend.

# VI

# THE ZAMBEZI MISSION FROM THE TURN OF THE CENTURY UNTIL THE FIRST WORLD WAR

## A. François Coillard's testament

A few days after the memorial service at the Oratory in Paris, the Board received from the district officer of Northern Rhodesia the will written by Coillard on 3 March 1903, on the eve of his journey to southern Africa, one article of which concerned the Paris Mission. "On the threshold of eternity and in the presence of my God, I solemnly bequeath to the churches of France, my native land, the responsibility of the Lord's work in the land of the Barotsis, and I plead with them, in his holy name, never to give it up; to do so would be a failure to recognise and reject the rich harvest awaiting the seeds that were sown through tears and suffering."

This unexpected and unusual document (even if Boegner probably knew of it) was a first in the history of mission. It is a dramatic illustration of Coillard's constant fear that the Zambezi Mission would escape from Paris Mission control, and that French Protestantism would ultimately lose interest. On writing this will, Coillard had three reasons to fear such a situation.

### The attraction of Ethiopianism in Europe

Certain circles had come to hear of Maurice Leenhardt's theories according to which Ethiopianism was caused, among other things, by "the errors, the lack of flexibility and lack of pedagogical abilities of some missionaries." Added to this, certain people, on reading the first letters of Coillard on the subject, as published in the JDME, were not far from thinking along the same lines as Leenhardt, and suggested that, instead of fighting Ethiopianism, it should be considered rather as an ally in the evangelisation of the Zambezi.

The Board was conscious of this trend among its readers, and on 1 April 1900, thought it necessary to issue a warning, which affirmed Coillard's point of view. The subject took up much of the Paris Mission President's report at the General Assembly on 25 April 1901. It was summed up in the JDME in May: "The President was at pains to spell out the danger of hastening the indigenous Church on the path of autonomy, and the lessons learnt, in this regard, from the Ethiopian movement."

Coillard's reaction to Leenhardt's book is unknown, but it is fairly certain that he knew of it when it was published in 1902. This would explain his fears that such ideas might lead French Protestantism to abandon the 'non-colonial' missions, of which the Zambezi Mission would have been the most vulnerable.

## A move to abandon the Zambezi

Coillard's fear of this was justified to some degree. During the second consultative conference of the sub-committees in Paris, 10-11 July 1902, the president, Pastor Pierre Dieterlen, read a letter from Gustave Steinheil of the Alsace committee. The letter proposed the creation of a new mission society in Geneva which would take over entire responsibility for the Zambezi Mission. Following a telegramme from Edouard Favre rejecting this solution, and a paper by Roger Hollard on 'Colonial and non-colonial missions', Steinheil's proposal was rejected unanimously and the assembly confirmed its unwavering support for the "Paris Mission in the fields of work entrusted to it by the Lord."

Although regularly rejected, the proposal to abandon the mission came onto the agenda regularly. Coillard knew this only too well, and despite his will, it would continue to come up at Board meetings.

## Lewanika did not come to France

In 1902, Lewanika was invited to England for the coronation of Edward VII. For a long time he had been hoping for such an invitation, but Coillard had tried to dissuade him from going to Europe, thinking him not up to sitting with kings and fearing the journey might add to his pride. Contacts between the two men were often stormy and, on Coillard's side, far from deferential. J.P. Burger writes: "Coillard spoke to Lewanika with a sometimes offensive frankness he was unaccustomed to from his courtiers. Lewanika, by affecting indifference, got his own back on Coillard, his so-called 'friend and counsellor'."

Lewanika's conversion involved countless visits from Coillard during which his pastoral counselling often turned into lectures on catechism, but to no avail. Before leaving the Lozi country for Europe in October 1895, the king had declared to the missionary: "Alas, if I am not yet saved, it isn't your fault. You have given yourself no respite but you've not given me any either."

Finally, Lewanika landed in England on 24 May 1902; Adolphe Jalla and Alfred Bertrand were there to welcome him. On seeing the public success of this visit and the numerous comments in the press, the Paris Board did everything it could to arrange for Lewanika to come to Paris, "to witness publicly, in the very place where those who had died for his people had come from, to the great work achieved in the name of Jesus." No effort was spared by the Board to try to get Lewanika across the Channel. On 29 May, an invitation with a letter of introduction from Jalla and Bertrand was sent to him through Joseph Chamberlain, the Secretary of State for Colonies. Then Georges Appia was delegated by the Board to represent it on 23 June at a reception given by the Bible Society in London.

Having heard that the Chartered Company and the British Government were not in favour of Lewanika's visit to France, the Board tried once more on 18 June to write to Chamberlain, underlining Lewanika's disappointment at not being able to visit Paris and insisting on the purely religious and moral nature of such a visit to those he called his fathers. Nothing came of it. Chamberlain did not reply and Lewanika did not come to France.

The Board was painfully surprised by all the political obstacles to this visit. Nevertheless, it felt some satisfaction on receiving a letter from Lewanika confirming that he had not forgotten his 'fathers and mothers'. He sent them a greeting 'in the name of the Lord', and... an appeal for missionary reinforcements. This letter was published in the JDME in September 1902, with a photograph taken in England of Lewanika holding a top-hat, sitting next to the Ngambela, together with two others from the Lozi delegation, plus Adolphe Jalla and Alfred Bertrand.

The mission friends in France could interpret these documents in two ways. The letter proved that Lewanika wanted the work of the Paris Mission to continue in the Lozi nation, but the photograph showed that the Protestants of France were totally left out of the Lozi missionary environment. Some mission friends might thus conclude that this Mission was no longer their affair, one of the reasons for Coillard's reminder in his will never to abandon the work.

As for the Board, it could no longer shrug off the responsibilities that Coillard had burdened it with over the past twenty years. On reading the will on 7 November 1904, the Board unanimously declared its agreement: "To enter fully into Coillard's line of thought and to maintain, as long as God will provide it with the means, the link established from the start between the Paris Mission Society and the work in the Zambezi."

## B. The aftermath – a heavy inheritance

Led by a single person for twenty years, the Zambezi Mission in 1904 inevitably entered the post-Coillard period. In the historiography of missions, it is said that Coillard's death left the mission 'kingless'. More than that, it was left in a critical situation after the break-up of the group of seventeen, and the settlement of the Ethiopians on the threshold of the capital, even if their undertaking would rapidly come to nothing.

The ensuing period, under the leadership of Adolphe Jalla, appointed president by the Conference at Lealui in September 1904, brought no change of direction. On the contrary, the strategy to create new stations and abandon others remained the order of the day. Schools, workshops and medical work continued, with the implementation of the health and sanitation methods established in 1900 and construction of healthier, prefabricated houses from Europe. The construction of river barges and the purchase of a motorboat rendered the Mission less dependent on the king's barges and the whims of the ferrymen.

To carry out his vast programme, supported actively by the hundred or so Zambezias in Europe, workers were needed. And, surprisingly, after the hecatomb of 1899-1900, numerous candidates continued to volunteer for the Zambezi. Between 1901 and 1906, no less than twenty-five people went out to work in the Zambezi, a period marked by no deaths apart from those of Coillard and Emma Jalla, in Italy following the birth of her third child.

As people could only travel in the Zambezi during the dry season, between April and June, it was during this period that each year, reinforcements arrived:

*1901*
- Albert and Julie Lageard, an Italian pastor with a German wife, were posted to Nalolo, a station that had been without a European occupant for three years.
- Françoise Glauser, a teacher from Bern was posted to the school at Sesheke but repatriated in 1904.
- Isabelle Roulet, a teacher from Neuchâtel, taught first at Lealui where the English section was finally set up, then at Sefula where in 1903 she married Juste Bouchet.
- Maurice Anker, with no particular appointment, was posted to the trade school at Sefula. He was repatriated a year later, after having built some flat-bottomed barges on the model of those used by the Swiss army. These were copied by his successor.

*1902*
- Georges and Elisabeth Volla, an Italian pastor and his Swiss wife, settled in Lealui.
- Georges Reutter, a Swiss doctor, and his wife Marguerite settled in Sesheke where he founded the medical mission of the Lower-

Zambezi. It was he who, in 1902, made an appeal for the establishment of a special fund for healthier housing. He promoted tropical hygiene, the preventive use of quinine, the wearing of pith helmets and the use of mosquito nets.

- Albert Champod, a Swiss artisan, posted first to Sefula, then to Nalolo.
- Hélène Bertrand, a French teacher, posted to Nalolo.
- Laure Nicole, a Swiss teacher, and Lea Rioux, a French deaconess, both posted to Sefula.

*1903*

- Gustave Berger, a Swiss pastor, and his wife Sara took over the station at Mabumbu, founded in 1899 to set up, away from the capital, a school to teach English and the future teacher-training college. This project had been abandoned by its European staff after the death of Eva de Prosch and the departure of Alfred and Maggie Mann following the latter's death. It was at Mabumbu that the Conference decided to found a second medical mission on the Upper-Zambezi, with Dr Roderich Prosch as director.
- Miss Kleinhaus from Switzerland arrived to join her fiancé, Albert Champod.
- Sophie Amez-Droz, a teacher from Neuchatel joined Elise Kiener at Lealui.
- Félix Vernet and Ernest Huguenin, French and Swiss artisans, settled at Seoma, between Sesheke and Senanga. The site seemed favourable for a hydraulic saw-mill to which the Sefula trade school was subsequently transferred.

Also, during his last visit to South Africa, Coillard had returned with three craftsmen enlisted on the spot for a three-year period: N.B. Simpson, John Brunner, M. Kleingiebel.

*1904*

- Emma Grétillat, a teacher from Neuchâtel was posted to Senanga, founded in 1898, and which had had no European staff since the departure on furlough of the Boiteuxs in 1902.
- John Roulet, brother of Isabelle Bouchet, was a Swiss craftsman posted to Sefula.
- Victor and Evangeline Ellenberger, related to the Christol and Ellenberger families from Lesotho, posted to Nalolo.
- S.J. Fort, a British teacher sent to the English school at Lealui.
- 1905: David Lescoute, a French artisan, sent with Théophile Burnier to open the first station in the West, twelve kilometres

inland from the right bank of the river, level with Lealui. This region was thought to be fertile and densely populated, and was set up to compensate for abandoning Kazungula definitively.

*1906*

- Nina Jalla from Italy, Louis Jalla's new wife.
- Jenny Bourquin, who arrived to join John Roulet, her fiancé.
- In addition to this list, in 1905 ten African fellow workers (with only one from Lesotho) came as evangelists to each station. One of them, Filipi Nyundo, was given responsibility for Mongu, a new station founded in 1904 between Mabumbu and Sefula.

In reviewing this panel of European personnel sent to the Zambezi Mission in the period just prior to and after its founder's death, it is noteworthy that the Swiss were in the majority (fourteen), and that most were men and women teachers and craftsmen (fifteen). Not a single French pastor had offered his services. The preponderance of Swiss was the result of the intense activity of the Zambezias of Switzerland in particular. It should be noted nevertheless that the Geneva secretariat worked in harmony with the Mission Board in Paris.

A double concern arose in 1906, not only in Paris and Geneva but across the Channel, where Catherine Mackintosh, Coillard's sister in-law, became the centre of British solidarity with the Zambezi. The first concern was connected with the general orientation of the Mission which confused many supporters in Switzerland and Great Britain. The second concern was the difficult state of finances in France after the separation of church and state.

At a meeting of the Zambezi Commission in March 1906, attended by Louis Jalla and his wife, Edouard Favre and Alfred Bertrand, the question of the general direction of the Mission was raised. Jalla had just returned from a trip to Lake Nyassa (now Malawi) and to Uganda, where he had visited Scottish mission stations. These had large numbers of staff and were well-equipped, compared with the Zambezi Mission stations. He had the feeling that in the Lozi country they were 'playing at being missionaries' (sic). He thought that the teaching and technical staff, however numerous and well-meaning, were insufficiently qualified, and that the new initiatives seemed to be going in all directions. Certain studies for important projects such as healthier housing and the saw-mill at Seoma had not been undertaken sufficiently seriously. On hearing this, Alfred Boegner added that in reading the missionary reports he had felt some uncertainty in the ideas on what to do, to adjust or to give up. He noted that the general tone was pessimistic, and that the information given was unclear and varied from one missionary to another.

Following on these discussions, the Commission decided, on Boegner's recommendation, to request the Zambezi Conference to provide a report laying out "their collective opinion on the work and their needs, so as to give a solid basis on which to build the work." They also insisted that "the Conference be made aware of the need to strengthen its internal organisational structures so as to ensure more cohesion and a clearer focus, indispensable for a successful continuance of its work."

It is evident that Boegner wanted to take matters in hand with regard to the Zambezi which, it should be noted, had not been possible during Coillard's life time. But before writing his letter, he first had to take the advice of the Board, preoccupied with a record deficit. As already noted, the effects of the separation of church and state in France were having a serious effect. The Society's accounts for the 1905 financial year showed a deficit of 260.000 Francs, a quarter of the general budget. The Zambezi accounts, though funded from abroad for three-quarters of their needs, were also in deficit.

At a Board meeting on 2 April 1906, the situation was examined; Adrien de Jarnac, supported by Eric de Bammeville, suggested that part of the Lesotho stations and some on the Lower Zambezi be ceded to English or Scottish missions so as to "bring the budget back to sensible limits, and to enable the work of evangelisation to continue in the French colonies." Once again, it was explained to these two gentlemen that as the larger part of Lesotho and Zambezi finances came from other countries, there was no guarantee that abandoning these two missions would ensure their budget was transferred to the 'colonial missions.' Finally the Board decided to maintain its "traditional policy which lent an ecumenical character to the Mission Society." But this was evidence that the opposition to 'non-colonial' missions persisted, even at the level of the Board, especially from those at some distance both geographically and theologically from the headquarters at Boulevard Arago in Paris.

On 11 April, Boegner was ready to write his letter to the Zambezi Conference asking them for a detailed report on the activities of the past twenty years. Each of the twenty-three pages was an attempt to identify the uneasiness which mission friends experienced with regard to the Zambezi Mission, and to give general advice on how to foster unity among the missionaries. For the future, the letter proposed strict rules on the functioning of the Mission. For example, the missionaries were asked to concentrate their energy on well-established stations, and to undertake no new ventures without the consent of the Board. "That during the period of its foundation" wrote Boegner "it was possible to act differently, by sowing and planting day-by-day – that we recognise. But that time is past..." Now, he continued "they had to work in depth. Care should be given to the training of indigenous workers, teachers and evangelists, while waiting for pastors of their own." Boegner quoted the suggestive title of a conference by Bishop Tucker of Uganda: "Self-extension, self-support and self-government in missionary Churches."

Several times, Boegner outlined a professional missionary ethic. He asked them, as he had suggested to the Zambezi Commission, to ensure that in their writings and letters, they should not let their concern with the truth degenerate into pessimism about events and human relations. Love should triumph over disparagement. He advised them also not to make individual appeals for assistance but to develop a sense of solidarity with other mission fields so as not to give the impression that the Zambezi benefited from a superfluity, when the needs of other fields were not satisfied.

The Mission Conference, held at Mabumbu in July 1906, set to work, Boegner's letter having given them the necessary framework. The report of this Conference appeared in extenso in the JDME in November 1906, and in the Nouvelles du Zambèze the same month. It was in three parts: the work accomplished, the present situation, the future.

It seemed clear that, despite some setbacks in public morality (an increase of alcoholism, ritual dances and theft in Lewanika's absence in Europe), the main signs of progress which could be attributed to the Mission concerned social questions. There had been no tribal wars since the foundation of the Mission, the last raid dating back to 1892. The slave trade was forbidden as from 1895. Raids on children and payment of tribute in the form of children were dying out. Emancipation of slaves was imminent; its proclamation in July 1896 was publicly announced by Adolphe Jalla. Women's status seemed to be improving; Christian women acquired the right of emancipation from their polygamous husbands and girls, victims of rape, could appeal to the king for protection. Poisoning, murder, witchcraft were severely punished and with the advent of the British administrator, the death sentence was abolished. Public security was assured throughout the country for Africans and Europeans alike.

However, the results of missionary work per se appeared very slim, thereby justifying Boegner's questions. School and church attendance had diminished since the king no longer put pressure on the population to attend. No reason is given for this, except that participation in the services seemed less linked than in the past to pressure from the traditional authorities. Was it a sign of a new understanding of the rights of the person and individual freedoms? Above all, the serious lack of local teachers was evident and, in the churches, the Lozi evangelists, like the missionaries, lacked mobility.

For the whole mission, statistics indicated forty-two baptised people. The report insisted on the fact that the missionaries had, up till now, thought it their duty "to be very exacting in accepting those requesting baptism, considering it wise to make the door of the church narrow for them." Some catechumens attended classes for twelve years before being admitted to baptism, a practice based on the Lesotho discipline. According to J.P. Burger, this explained the slow progress of the church. "Baptism had become the final achievement of perfect people, instead of the starting point of a Christian in the making," he wrote.

As to the religious future of the work, the report noted that after a dispute between Willie Mokalapa and Lewanika, the Ethiopian movement had collapsed and, for the moment, disappeared. Trust between the Lozi population and the Mission seemed to have been restored and therefore the Conference decided to maintain the existing stations and even envisaged setting up new outposts directly linked to these stations.

On this subject, Boegner's recommendation of consolidating the current stations was not taken account of, but as any extension was linked to the granting of additional funds and the (most unlikely) arrival of reinforcements, it is to be concluded that it was more wishful thinking than a realistic project. In fact, forced by budgetary considerations, the consolidation did eventually occur. The new station at Semoa was abandoned in 1907 and the stations of Nalolo, Sesheke and Senanga went through periods of neglect. In the end, of the ten stations initially founded, eight became permanent and, after the war, were supplemented with annexes.

On reading the important 1906 report, one realises that the generation of missionaries still in the field had some difficulty in quitting the heroic pioneer mindset that had characterised the work up to Coillard's death and beyond. This would remain the case as long as the many reinforcements of the 1900-1906 period continued to give the illusion that the occupation of the country was still the order of the day. It was thanks to renewed contacts with the Lesotho Mission that the Zambezi Mission was finally able to define more accurately the nature of its vocation, to set a limit for its work, and to find the indispensable means for its development: a teacher-training college and a school for evangelists.

## C. Renewed contacts with the Lesotho Mission

The Ethiopian crisis over and the financial difficulties of the Paris Mission seeming to be long-term, it is understandable that the Zambezi Conference should turn again to Lesotho. During his last visit to the country in 1903, Coillard had suggested that Sotho pastors, rather than evangelists, might be sent to work in the Lozi country. Juste Bouchet had repeated this idea to his colleagues in 1906, on returning from leave, and suggested that a delegation from Lesotho come to study the question of this Sotho-Lozi collaboration. Thus, at the Sesheke Conference in 1907, five people arrived from Lesotho: Hamilton and Aline Dyke, principals of the Teacher-training College in Morija, the new director of the Morija Bible School, Frédéric Christol, the first person to offer his services for the Zambezi in 1879 and Georges Balzer, a Lesotho missionary since 1904.

At the end of this meeting, Dyke having rejected the idea of sending once again to the Zambezi evangelists to be employed as teachers, he suggested that his colleagues open their own teacher-training college. So, on 5 November 1907, the Mabumbu Teacher-training College opened its doors with Auguste Coïsson at its head. As for the plan of sending Sotho pastors, the Lesotho delegation did not think it wise. In view of the basic level of evangelisation of the Lozi communities, these Sotho pastors, who exercised semi-episcopal responsibilities in Lesotho, would see it as a demotion. However, it offered to propose to the Lesotho missionary council that a new attempt be made to send Sotho evangelists. They would try to avoid the mistakes of the past, by limiting the length of their stay and by ensuring they would not be under the orders of the missionaries.

In view of past difficulties, it was important that the matter be discussed in the Lesotho consistories. It finally appeared on the agenda of the Seboka (mixed conference of pastors and missionaries) on 18 October 1908, which concluded the celebration of the 75th anniversary of the Lesotho Mission. An important delegation had come from the Lozi country for the celebration including Adolphe Jalla and Emile Boiteux, with two evangelist students, Josepha Imasiksoana and Francis Illutombi, Prince Litia and two of his chiefs. Several times, the visitors from the Zambezi appealed for help for their country, recalling that it was the Sotho evangelists and French missionaries who were the first to reach their country. In his speech, Litia identified himself as 'a child of Lesotho through his education' and pleaded, after having been thus nurtured by them, that his people not be abandoned by the Sothos.

In his report of the discussions at Seboka in the JDME, Jean Bianquis, known for his reservations about the Zambezi Mission, nevertheless admired their forthright spirit: "When past mistakes are openly recognised and confessed, when one places at the forefront the will to accomplish God's work, and to hasten the coming of his Kingdom, no obstacle is insurmountable... everyone agreed to resume the collaboration."

These renewed contacts between the two missions could not but gladden Boegner whose missiological reflections had led him, in the first weeks following his nomination as director of the Paris Mission, to define the missionary task of the church. It is not surprising therefore to find him writing in the JDME of January 1909 lines which could have been written forty years earlier, when Coillard believed that the Lesotho Church would give birth to the Church of the Zambezi: "This Zambezi Mission is the genuine daughter, the rightful heir to the work accomplished in Lesotho, with the undeniable differences of time and space, under infinitely more difficult conditions than those met by the Lesotho pioneers. The Zambezi Mission had in common with its predecessor profoundly identical inspirations, methods and general conditions of development, despite some outward differences... In a word, if we are faithful, everything leads us to believe that our French Protestantism has already acquired, on the banks of the Zambezi, a second Lesotho." Yet, once again, this grand vision of the development of mission would be aborted through circumstances which Boegner might consider of secondary importance but which often interfere with the best laid plans and affect the course of history.

Five Sotho evangelists set out for the Zambezi Mission between 1910 and 1912. But death and disease struck them cruelly and in 1914, it was decided to end the collaboration between the two missions. Jeriele Theko placed at Sefula in 1910 died of black-water fever in 1911. Jakobo Makakole placed at Nalolo in 1910, had to be repatriated due to his wife's health. He was replaced by Oziase Mafubetswana in 1911, who asked to be sent home in January 1913, as did Nikodema Tsiu after a short stay at Nalolo between 1912 and 1913. Joele Mofolo, who had been sent as a Sotho teacher to Livingstone, after the death of the evangelist Petrosi Kasale, only stayed from 1911 to 1914 before returning to Lesotho.

# VII

## CONCLUDING REMARKS
### A LAST LOOK AT THE ZAMBEZI MISSION BEFORE THE
### 1914-1918 WAR

The failure of the renewed co-operation of the two missions was not the only difficulty met in Lozi country. A number of the reinforcements who had come since 1907 were unable to continue their work and a series of departures of the older and more experienced among them made matters worse.

On 18 June 1909, Théodore Fuhrmann, an Italian missionary who had come to Lealui two years earlier, died of malaria. In 1909, Dr Prosch, replaced for two years by a colleague from Geneva, Dr Troendlé, left on leave after ten years of service. On the way home, he died in Uganda on 27 February 1910 of a malignant tumour. Soon after, in March 1912, Dr Reutter suggested closing the medical station at Sesheke to allow Mabumbu to be maintained while waiting for a replacement for Dr Troendlé, who had returned to Switzerland. When the Reutters left definitively in March 1912, Anna Saucon, a French trained nurse who had arrived in 1911, was left to run the Zambezi Medical mission on her own.

That same year, Franck Escande of Sefula, the son of Elisée Escande of Madagascar, the first French pastor to Zambezi since the death of Coillard, was allowed to go to Switzerland to see his fiancée Anna Grob who was dangerously ill. She died the following year and, in September 1914, Franck Escande who had intended to return to the Zambezi, was mobilised and soon killed in the trenches of Northern France.

It seems the Zambezi Mission was unable to keep its French pastors. Frank Christol, posted in 1911 to Lukona then Mabumbu, and Robert Dieterlen (1912 – Lukona then Sefula), both sons of Lesotho missionaries, were reclaimed by the Mission. Christol, together with the craftsman Felix Vernet, was sent to help out in Cameroon and Dieterlen, mobilised in 1914, died in the trenches of Artois on 25 September 1915. Personal and other difficulties among the teaching staff, added to the problems mentioned above, led the Board in Paris to send Alfred Casalis out for a year.

At Boegner's death in February 1912, Alfred Casalis became the General Secretary of the Paris Mission. He was the son of Eugène Casalis, the Lesotho pioneer and was sent to the Zambezi because "the Mission friends had long been preoccupied by the evident weakening of that mission field." The Board was aware that in him they had found the right man to encourage the workers "to be strong in a spirit of brotherly unity and consecration, the hallmark from the start of the Lesotho Mission."

What was all this really about? In fact, the trouble had been caused by a 'culpable' liaison between Johanna Dietrich, a German teacher recruited by the German Zambezias in 1911, and Ernest Huguenin, a craftsman who had arrived 1903 and had married Emma Gretillat in 1906. By the end of Alfred Casalis' stay in 1914, the three people concerned had left the country. For personal reasons, David Lescoute, a craftsman and Alice Fabre, a teacher who had arrived in 1910, both returned home to France. All these departures contributed to the weakening of the Mission.

What is of most interest is Casalis' general evaluation of the Mission. No official report exists, but his impressions were noted in several letters to the Board, some of which were published in the JDME in 1913 and 1914 and in a booklet called 'Croquis du Zambèze' (Sketches from the Zambezi) published for the Mission friends. Jean-Paul Burger has summed these up in 'Notes on the history of the Zambezi Church'. The three main points are:

## Inappropriate methods of evangelisation
He noted that the Zambezi Mission, after 30 years, could hardly count more than 200 conversions. He compared this with the neighbouring Plymouth Brethren Mission led by Arnot, that had converted several thousand people.

Casalis felt sure the difference was due to a lack of method. He criticised the system of a chain of mission stations, too numerous and too large, and all efforts to strengthen them to the detriment of evangelisation. According to him, this system had led to the promotion of an elite in the Lozi nation to the detriment of the masses. To reach the latter, annexes led by local workers should be set up. As to the foreign missionaries, certainly some ordained, dedicated, strong and enterprising missionaries were needed, but Casalis thought that "our young missionaries badly need to 'think black'". He considered that "what was lacking the most in some of our work was neither courage, nor sacrifice, nor activity, nor intelligence but method" (letter to J. Bianquis on 4 February 1914).

J.P. Burger regretted that, after his departure in 1914, Casalis did not return to the Zambezi, as the Board had suggested. It would have hastened the change in methods that only came after 1930.

**The Sotho language was not understood by the majority**

This was a subject discussed by the missionaries a number of times and on which they were not unanimous. The Sotho language brought into the Lozi country by the Kololo had, over the past century, been considerably modified and diversified, so that the spoken language in the region no longer corresponded to the literary Sotho used in the mission schools and in the churches, in Bibles and hymn books.

Some missionaries were convinced that, in order to evangelise the ethnic groups, each with its own language, it was necessary to use one language understood by all, i.e. Sesotho. Eugène Béguin, for instance, wrote in the JDME in 1902 "it is an absurd legend" to believe that missionaries do not want to learn the Lozi language. According to him, Sotho, like French, should prevail over the regional languages. The question of abandoning Sesotho was discussed in the famous report of 1906, but no decision was taken at the time.

Alfred Casalis was for abandoning it. As soon as he arrived at Sesheke on 10 August 1912, he wrote: "I am beginning to have doubts about the use of Sesotho in Barotseland. Is it as well understood as the founders thought it was? This is not certain. In any case, today, people speak Sikololo to one another, a sort of Sotho dialect, but which is sufficiently different not to be understood by an untrained ear. Sikololo is certainly the language our young missionaries should adopt. The time has come to fix its spelling and syntax and to start its use in the schools and the church."

In spite of some opposition at the Missionary Conference, this point of view was adopted, and Adolphe Jalla set about putting together the first publication in the Lozi language: an alphabet and a geography text book in 1914, a reader in 1915, an English-Lozi dictionary in 1917, and after the war the Gospels.

**Church discipline was too rigid**

When the missionary Arnot passed through Lealui in February 1914, Casalis was amazed to hear that the Plymouth Brethren were far less strict in their church discipline compared to the Church of Zambezi. Polygamists were admitted to the church on condition that they did not take new wives and that they take measures to free their other wives where possible. On 15 February he wrote to the Board in Paris: "It seems that we are the only ones applying the severe discipline that used to be prevalent in all our mission fields, based on the Lesotho example... In fact, we worked from the idea of a Church of Saints. But there are no such churches on this earth. The Church is our Alma Mater, the school where our souls learn to walk in the path of holiness. The church is not an end in itself, it is a means, a path, a mother who nurtures her children... How important it is that missionaries be great hearted, intelligent and open-minded. In the mission field, narrow-mindedness suffocates life rather than creating it!"

Jean-Paul Burger notes that these reflections, though sent to the Board, were never communicated to the Conference. He wonders why and regrets it: "Perhaps were they afraid of fomenting divisions in the Conference and creating trouble among the small Christian communities, already affected by a certain legalism. Looking back, one can only regret the missed opportunity to re-examine the discipline as a whole in the light of Casalis' remarks. Because the church, instead of marking time, would have seen its growth accelerated by a better understanding of a major problem."

# THE PARIS MISSION: HOW VALID WERE THE ARGUMENTS TO MAINTAIN ITS WORK IN THE BRITISH COLONIES?

The Paris Mission initiated its work in Southern Africa at the outset of the colonial conquest, at a time when the political destiny of the Sotho and Lozi people was not yet sealed. Although the Cape Colony passed under the control of Great Britain in 1815, the inclusion of these two peoples in its sphere of influence was only gradually felt. The sovereignty of the Sotho kingdom was on several occasions almost destroyed by the Boers. It was only in 1884 that Great Britain decided definitively to grant a protectorate to Moshoeshoe. For a time, control of the Lozi country was disputed between the British and the Portuguese, and it only became a British Protectorate in 1897, exercised through the British South African Mining Company, covering the peoples in the British Zambezi (ex-Northern Rhodesia, now Zambia).

These transformations, occurring while the Paris Mission was already installed in the region, did not provoke politico-religious crises similar to those the mission had met in Gabon, in Algeria and in an acute form in the Pacific fields. Not only were the non-British Protestant missionaries (French, Swiss, Italians) never bothered by the British authorities, but were associated with them on occasion. Eugène Casalis in 1842, Adolphe Mabille in 1883 and François Coillard in 1889, at the request of Moshoeshoe and Lewanika respectively, assisted in the official process leading to the establishment of the protectorates.

What is the explanation for the cordial relations between the British authorities and the foreign missionaries when relations between the French authorities and foreign missionaries were so tense elsewhere? Several factors can be noted:

- The religion of the foreign missionaries was that of the majority in Britain. In southern Africa, the British colonial authorities were faced with French, Swiss and Italian missionaries belonging to a well-established and respected denomination. Things were different for France, where in the Pacific and Madagascar the missionaries were of a different confession and were considered as rivals.

- Interaction between the British colonial authorities and French Protestant missionaries did not occur at a time of diplomatic crisis between the two mother countries. Indeed, the protection granted by

Great Britain to Lesotho and Zambezi was never seriously contested, and certainly not by France. By contrast, the French colonial authorities generally encountered British missionaries in the context of a transfer of sovereignty, and the French saw them as agents of British imperialism. This was not always unfounded and they felt it necessary to get rid of them so as to confirm their own authority. Casalis and his successors could hardly be seen in the same light by the British.

- Protestant missions played an important civilising role in the precolonial period. This was duly recognised in colonial times.

The British tradition of non-separation of church and state facilitated the social role of missions and church practice as a whole, whereas France was involved at the time in a process of secularisation. Nevertheless, it should be noted that it was the non-conformist missions, (the London Missionary Society, the Methodist mission), independent of the state, which in both southern Africa and in the Pacific, played to the full a civilising role through their experimental administration of these 'new' countries. The Protestant missionaries of the Paris Mission Society, particularly those of the second generation, were quite at ease with the inheritance of the London Missionary Society, as many came from either Free churches or were closely linked with them.

- The missionaries of the Paris Mission were very loyal vis-à-vis Britain, adapting easily to the language and appreciating its culture and traditions. This loyalty was evident in all their dealings with the authorities. As in Lesotho and the Zambezi, British authority was the best placed to govern, they had no problems with assisting in its establishment and strengthening and respecting it. The importance of the role played by Casalis, Mabille and Coillard in the accession of the British protectorates should be underlined. A similar role was played by the Paris Mission in Madagascar and the Pacific: to assist the western powers to exercise their authority in matters of law and justice. Such was the concept of Christian loyalty for the missionaries of the Paris Mission.

It is worth noting that these missionaries found themselves in an unusual situation, different to that of their British Protestant fellow-missionaries or their French Catholic opposite numbers. It is hard to imagine either group working to bring about the protectorate of the other country. There is no doubt that the missionaries of the Paris Mission, whose headquarters were in Paris but whose network of staff and friends was international, constituted a new type of worker beyond national and ecclesiastical boundaries. This seemed to foreshadow, long before its time, a European unity of churches and nations.

Perhaps it was precisely this situation that the Mission Board had such difficulty in getting across to French Protestantism, of which the majority was unaware of the privileged position offered by the Mission de Paris. The directors of the Paris Mission, under Alfred Boegner, had valiantly defended the position that French Protestantism should not give up its non-colonial missions (Lesotho-Zambezi) to other foreign societies. There were three main reasons:

- An indestructible covenant had been established in the past between the Sotho and French nations, an alliance extended to the Lozi people (cf. Coillard's will).

- The extension of the Lesotho Mission to the Zambezi; the two missions constituted a reservoir of experience for other mission fields and the national churches.

- The effort to maintain the international and interdenominational character of French mission, a source of strength and originality from the start.

How valid were these three arguments for the maintenance of the Paris Mission in the British colonial sphere? The idea that Lesotho and the Zambezi should never be abandoned due to the spiritual links uniting the French, Sotho and Lozi people was no doubt theologically justified by the human and financial sacrifices asked of, and granted by, French Protestants in these two mission fields. But, as noted earlier, these alliances were established back in the past by individuals supported by a minority of French Protestants; the majority were unaware of most of what was happening so far away. Casalis and Coillard certainly acted in the name of all French Protestants, and neither hesitated to make such a claim both orally or in writing, particularly Coillard. However, the message only really reached the network of friends of the Mission, hardly at all elsewhere. The fact that a considerable percentage of French Protestants would have seen no major problem in breaking the spiritual links with the Sotho and Lozi to the benefit of those in the French colonies is shown notably by two things:

- First, French Protestantism in general did not see its role as a 'mother-church' with 'daughter' churches throughout the world to which it would send missionaries.

- Also, it was not convinced that the experiences of evangelisation and of church establishment in Lesotho and the Zambezi could contribute much to its own church life. For it, mission remained to a certain extent a question of the 'foreign affairs' of the church, with little impact on its own internal affairs. The missionary argument, a constant concern of

Boegner's, that mission was part of the structure of the church, had continually to be repeated.

For the Paris Mission, to give up Lesotho and the Zambezi would mean, in some ways, depriving itself of the 'the goose that lays the golden eggs'. As noted earlier, despite the setbacks and disavowals, the directors and missionaries of the Paris Mission, Boegner and Coillard in particular, were unwavering in their efforts to apply to the Zambezi the well-tried methods used in Lesotho. But as also noted, there were limits to the Sotho model, itself based on the 'ma'ohi' method used by the London Missionary Society, and several aspects were totally inappropriate to the Zambezi context. After the death of Coillard, the Paris Mission had not been able to identify rapidly new models or set up new missionary strategies better adapted to the specific situation in the country. Alfred Casalis' 1913 analyses, only picked up ten years later by Maurice Leenhardt, led to the hope that after the war, the African Missions might cease to be the model for all the others.

It is extremely likely, finally, that if the Paris Mission had withdrawn from Lesotho and the Zambezi, it would have lost the major part of its support and funds from Switzerland and Italy, which would have still been spent on mission through other channels. It is also probable that a good part of the funds collected by the French free churches would not have gone to the 'colonial' missions of the Paris Mission in view of the internationalist spirit which had been growing in church circles. Deprived of these two sources of funds, the Paris Mission would no doubt have become a Society essentially for the Reformed fraction of French Protestantism. This amputation (of Lesotho and the Zambezi) would not have drawn in more liberals, because of the theological disagreements with the conservative majority on the Board, nor more Lutherans, fervent supporters of the Norwegian mission.

As to the spheres of influence and global visibility of French Protestantism, its presence in Lesotho and the Zambezi was a considerable asset in terms of international relations. But it must be noted that on the cusp of the two centuries, French Protestantism had not fully comprehended its role on the international scene, no doubt because the French Protestant Federation had not yet fully established itself.

It would be in the framework of international missionary conferences that the Paris Mission would ultimately find the international openings enabling French Protestantism to gain awareness of its place in the universal church, before the war once again momentarily closed the doors.

IMPRIMERIE
LUSSAUD
OFFSET & NUMERIQUE

L'impression et le façonnage
de cet ouvrage
ont été effectués
à l'Imprimerie LUSSAUD
85200 Fontenay-le-Comte

Dépôt légal 4ᵉ trimestre 2004
n° 3810
N° d'impression : 203779